A STAY AT HOME DAD'S GUIDE TO RAISING EXTRAORDINARY KIDS

Dr. Jon Kester

authorHOUSE®

AuthorHouse™
1663 Liberty Drive
Bloomington, IN 47403
www.authorhouse.com
Phone: 833-262-8899

Published by AuthorHouse 01/06/2022

ISBN: 978-1-6655-4859-5 (sc)
ISBN: 978-1-6655-4858-8 (e)

Library of Congress Control Number: 2022900344

Print information available on the last page.

DEDICATION

This book is dedicated to my parents who still to this day
are devoted to helping me be an extraordinary person.

CONTENTS

Congratulations to all the men and women out there who are blessed to be called parents and who take the time to care about how their children grow up. There is no greater privilege in life than bringing a tiny new human into this world and then trying to raise him or her properly during their childhood. Being a parent means to raise a child with the utmost love and passion so they can have a successful life. Parents must take into account that raising extraordinary kids requires all the intelligence, wisdom, and determination they will be able to muster.

This book will help you become a wiser, more determined parent with the easy to follow month by month parenting plan. A solid, intact parenting strategy will have a significantly positive impact on a child's present and future wellbeing and offers countless benefits for both parents and children. In fact children who grow up in homes where parents have strategies for success are less likely to experience a wide range of problems (academic, social, emotional, cognitive), not only in childhood but later on in adulthood as well (Amato; Howard & Reeves 2018,). In families with parenting strategies, children typically have access to more of the economic and community resources because parents are able to pool their time, money and energy; children tend to be more of the focus of the home.

Children living with a mom and dad who have parenting strategies are more often involved in community activities, take part in academic pursuits in local schools and other academic institutions that can lead to college, and eventually, a career. Children with parents who strive for them to be extraordinary with a plan have the highest high school and college graduation rates, as well as high employment rates according to a study by Harvard University. Being raised in a family where parents are directly involved in the child's life reduced a child's probability of living in poverty by about 82 percent. (2018 PEW Research)

In order for parents to see our kids become extraordinary we must be involved and have a plan. Remember being an involved parent takes time and is hard work, and it often means rethinking and rearranging our priorities. It frequently means sacrificing what you want to do for what your child needs to do. We must be there for our children both mentally as well as physically.

Being involved in your kid's life has many rewards—memories, great conversations, a deeper relationship with your child and the chance to watch your child grow into a healthy, responsible adult. Keep in mind that the more involved you are, the more valued your kids feel, and the more likely they'll be to respond to you.

One of the biggest challenges facing parents when it comes to being more involved with their child is figuring out how. The involvement can take many forms which all will be discussed in the upcoming chapters in this book. Parental actions such as being a role model, instilling good habits, being consistent in discipline, and building good relationships. This can be done by taking quality time out of our day to nurture your relationship with the children in your life with both grace and love. The key for this books success is being able to spend quality time with your kids. What is quality time? As long as you as a parent are communicating with your child in an upbeat and useful way, you are spending quality time with them. Just being in the same room as your children doesn't count. Here are some helpful ways to increase the amount of quality time you share with your child:

Establish together time.

Establish a regular weekly routine of doing something special with your child. Going out for a walk, getting some ice cream, or even having a conversation while you're cleaning up after dinner can help you open your lines of communication. This is essential to raising extraordinary children.

Have regular family meetings.

Family meetings provide a useful forum for sharing triumphs, complaints, projects and any other topics with each other. Establish some ground rules, such as everyone gets a chance to talk without interruption, and only constructive feedback is allowed. To get resistant children to join in, try using incentives like post-meeting ice cream.

Eat meals together as often as you can.

Family meal time provides a great opportunity to talk about the day's events, to unwind, reinforce and bond with your kids. Studies show again and again the significant, measurable scientific proof about the positive, lifelong benefits of family meals. Family meals nourish the spirit, brain and health of all family members. Regular family meals are linked to higher grades and self-esteem. Children who grow up sharing family meals are more likely to exhibit prosocial behavior as adults, such as sharing, fairness and respect. According to a Harvard University study (2018), with each additional family meal shared each week, adolescents are less likely to show symptoms of violence, depression and suicide, less likely to use or abuse drugs or run away, and less likely to engage in risky behavior or delinquent acts. Also both adults and children who eat at home more regularly are less likely to suffer from obesity.

Once you have the basic ideas of how to spend quality time with your children you are ready to take the next step of adding a specific parenting plan into your daily life. This book when used properly will be an amazing stepping stone into having extraordinary kids.

How to use this book

If you wish to get the most out of this book, there is one indispensable requirement and that to have a deep, driving desire to raise extraordinary kids and vigorous determination to increase your ability to parent.

This book is written with a plan for raising extraordinary kids on a monthly basis. I encourage you to read each month rapidly at first to get a bird's eye view of the concepts and then go back and reread each section thoroughly each month and apply one or two of the concepts from the chapter to your family. Be sure to stop frequently in your reading to think over what you are reading. Ask yourself just how and when you can apply each concept to your parenting.

Read this book with a pencil, pen, magic marker, or crayon in your hand. When you come across an idea that you feel you can use, circle it or make a note by it. It is perfectly fine to write ideas down on this book or underline important sentences.

If you want to get a real, lasting benefit out of this book don't imagine that skimming through it once will suffice. After reading thoroughly, you ought to spend some time reviewing it every month. Remember that the use of these concepts can be made habitual only by a constant and vigorous review and application.

We as parents must also remember that learning is an active process. We learn by doing. So, if you desire to be a better parent and raise extraordinary kids then you must apply the concepts from this book every opportunity that you get. If you don't you will forget them quickly and nothing will be improved in your child's life. It's important to understand that attempting new ideas in your family's lifestyle will require time and persistence and daily application. Remember that understanding the role of a parent takes time. Every person has the potential to be a great parent. It does not come overnight. Also when considering the responsibilities of parenting, it's important to remember that no one is perfect. We are all human and, at times, we do make mistakes. But the important thing to teach is: we can learn by our mistakes and try to avoid making the same mistakes over-and-over again. Remember that *"Parenting is not a challenge to be solved, but a reality to be experienced"*

CHAPTER 1

JANUARY

"It is easier to build strong children than to repair broken men." – Frederick Douglass

The month of January is all about a fresh start to the year; it's about new beginnings for you and your family. One of your New Year's resolutions should be to start raising extraordinary kids. This month starts out with three very important ideas (not raising victims, being dependable and having discipline) that will lay the ground work for your children growing up amazing. It will take a lot of dedication for these concepts to be incorporated into everyday life. So start now and have these values resonate for the rest of your child's days.

Don't Raise Victim's

There is a reason that the first recommendation on raising extraordinary kids is to make sure your children don't have a victim mentality. This in my opinion is one of the most important lessons we as parents MUST teach are children. The reason for the highest most importance for this is that when children have a victim mentality they are being held back from achieving their true potential, success, and happiness.

Here's the biggest fact: kids are only victims when parents allow them to be victims. In order for your child to be a victim, parents have to accept their excuses or their blame. I suggest that parents challenge your child's thinking by making sure they are not blaming others actions for their own. Remember, we as parents must not allow our children ever to think they are victims and make sure they alone take responsibility for their actions.

It's important for your child to know that failing a spelling test or missing free throws in the basketball game doesn't make them a victim. Our kids must understand that failure, rejection, and disappointment are part of life.

We as parents must help our children learn to take personal responsibility for the way they thinks, feels, and behaves. This is so that our kids don't go through life insisting they are victims of "mean" people and unfortunate circumstances.

Here are six steps parents can take to empower their children and make them lose the victim mentality:

1. Create "Gratefulness" Rituals

Being gratefulness keeps self-pity at bay. Spend time talking about what you're thankful for every day. Even when you encounter difficult circumstances, parents need to be role models of an appreciative attitude.

Create daily rituals that will help your child recognize all the reasons they have to be grateful. Here are a few ideas:

- At dinner, ask your child about the three favorite things that happened in school that day that they are appreciative for.
- At bedtime, ask them to tell you what the best part of their day was.
- Put pictures on the refrigerator that shows people and events that you as a family are thankful for.

2. Teach Your Child to Silence their Destructive Thinking

Some kids tend to have a more pessimistic outlook than others. But with a little help, they can recognize their negative thinking may not be accurate.

Help your child silence their negative thinking by looking for exceptions to the rule. If they insists, "I don't ever get to do anything fun," remind them of the fun activities they recently participated in. If your child says, "No one ever likes me," point out people who do. Remember as a parent your attitude is often times reflexed on to your child's thinking and now will be a good time to self-evaluate to make sure your outlook on life is positive.

3. Teach Your Child How to Deal with Unpleasant Emotions

Teach your child how to deal with uncomfortable emotions, like fear, anxiety, anger, and sadness. According to Dr. Diana Paulson, a child phycologist found that Kids who have healthy coping skills are less likely to insist on minor events are catastrophic.

Discipline your child's behavior, but not the emotion. Let your children know that their emotions are OK, but that it's important to handle those emotions in appropriate manners. Our children need to know healthy ways to express their feelings and not always have their own pity party every time they get upset.

A child who has confidence in their ability to handle disappointment won't lament that life isn't fair when it's time to leave the playground, or when they don't make the basketball team.

4. Teach Problem-Solving Skills

According to David Owens from the National institute of learning, Kids who lack problem-solving skills are likely to take a passive approach to life. A child who doesn't know how to do their math homework may resign to a failing grade without even trying to find a solution. Or, a child who doesn't make the soccer team may conclude they are a terrible athlete.

As parents we must teach our child how to problem-solve. A child who takes action when they face hardship is much less likely to see themselves as a helpless victim. Remember that kids with good problem-solving skills can prevent small stumbling blocks from turning into major obstacles.

5. Help Other People

It's easy for kids to think they have the biggest problems in the world. Showing them that there are plenty of other people with bigger problems can help them see that everyone faces hardships. Helping other people can show your child that no matter how young they are, or no matter what problems they experienced, they have the ability to help someone else.

Volunteer at a homeless shelter, help an elderly neighbor with yard work or participate in a fundraising project. Get your child involved in community service activities on a regular basis so they can recognize opportunities to make the world a better place.

6. Teach Assertiveness Skills

As parents we must teach our child that they don't have to be a passive victim. If another child grabs a toy from their hand, help them ask for it back. Or, if they are being picked on by other kids at school, talk about how to ask a teacher for help.

Kids with assertiveness skills can speak up and say, "Don't do that," or "I don't like it when you do that." Empower your child to use their words and you'll reduce the likelihood that they become a victim.

Conclusion

We as parents need to know that when children take on a victim mentality, it becomes a form of defiance, used to avoid taking appropriate responsibility for their actions. If left unchanged, the victim mentality can eventually impact your child's ability to have healthy relationships and to adequately function as an adult. It is vital that your child learn the skills discussed in this section in order to manage their accountability in the real world.

Discipline your kids

While taking a break from writing this book I took my kids to a local park. After sitting on a bench for only a few minutes I was shocked to observe a child who was literally out of control, he was doing everything from kicking kids bikes over, to trying to get the swings stuck on a tree, to taking a lid from a garbage can and throwing like a Frisbee into a shelter building. This child was doing this all well his mom just sat on a picnic table and said nothing about his behavior. All I could think of was how this poor kid needs discipline. After all, parents who hold back on giving children boundaries or firmly (but lovingly) correcting bad behavior may actually be harming their child with good intentions. According to Yale's adolescent studies professor David Foster, "Children who are not disciplined are unpleasant, selfish, and surprisingly unhappy." So in order to raise extraordinary kids we must discipline our children. Children who are given clear rules, boundaries, and expectations are responsible, more self-sufficient, are more likely to make good choices which benefits all of us in society when they are adults. Remember that discipline isn't just about giving kid's consequences. Instead, it ensures children are gaining the skills they need to become responsible adults. Children who have been given firm but loving discipline also have the following traits and abilities:

- They have more self-control and are more self-sufficient.
- They are more responsible and enjoy "being good" and helping others at home, at school and in the world at large.

- They are more self-confident. They know their opinions and feelings will be heard, and that their parents love them even when they make mistakes.
- They know that they are accountable for their mistakes or misbehavior, and are more likely to make good choices because they want to, not because they fear punishment.
- They are pleasant to be around and are more likely to have an easier time making friends.

Effective child discipline techniques using instruction:

As parents we must be sure to have effective discipline methods which mean having a plan of action. The first step in this successful discipline plan of action is for parents to state boundaries which are clearly and concisely defined and enforced. Also remember, as parents, we cannot flip-flop when children try to bargain or negotiate.

The second step to successful discipline is to deliver instructions calmly, yet steadfastly, not as a quivering request. It is more effective to say, "Do not run in a busy parking lot." Instead of "daddy needs you to stay by him in the parking lot, ok?" Children must know when parents are serious. Our authority must be clearly, consistently established. Use only the necessary words, and teach your children to develop eye contact and listening skills.

We as parents need to teach children good and moral behaviors by displaying your own good and moral behaviors. This could mean going to church as a family or picking up trash from around a park. Be sure to plan healthy family activities that promote good morals and together time. Your children will soon mirror your values and morals. According to Mayo clinic's head of Adolescents behavior, Tom Engram, child discipline and training does not occur in a vacuum. Their behaviors are formed within the context of what they witness in their primary teachers.

Conclusion:

Remember that discipline is not about creating conflict with your child or lashing out in anger. Child discipline, when done correctly, is not about trying to control your child but about showing them how to control their own behavior. It is not about punishing a child for doing something wrong but about setting clear boundaries and consequences for breaking rules so that they learns how to discipline him or herself.

A child who has been taught right from wrong and has a solid sense of what is negative and positive behavior will know when they have done something wrong. The goal is to have your child want to behave correctly out of a desire to be a good citizen and a member of their family and society—not because they fears punishment. So make your kids extraordinary and discipline your children.

Teach Kid's how to be Dependable

The final concept for the month of January is to teach your kids to be dependable. Having your kids be dependable means that others can rely on them, and that they follow through on promises they make. As parents we must make sure our children can be depended upon by their family, friends, and the greater community.

Children learn how to be dependable from having parents who they can count on. This means as a parent if you say you're coming home for dinner, do your best to be there. When you make a promise, try to fulfill it. If unexpected events keep you from following up, explain why honestly and simply. Here a few ways that both parents and children can work together to become more extraordinary through dependability.

Give Kids a Role in the Family

Let kids know that their contribution helps the family. Little by little, give your child chores that they are responsible for. Start with easy things, like setting the table and feeding pets. As time goes on, kids can move on to vacuuming a room and doing laundry. They might even help plan a family trip and do internet research on activities for weekend fun. Whatever they do, praise children for being responsible and let them know what they do is valued.

Help Them Get Organized

One of the biggest reasons that kids and adults alike are not dependable is because they have competing responsibilities. Between homework, chores, afterschool sports, and other responsibilities, kids may get overwhelmed or simply forget what they were supposed to do. Teach basic organization skills. For instance, have kids make a "to do" list with due dates and a general idea of how long each task will take.

Make a rule such as "homework first, video games after." Kids need to set daily goals and break long-term projects into chunks. If they get in the habit of checking their "to do" list or calendar each day and looking ahead, it will keep things from falling off their radar and make them way more dependable.

Be Patient

Hard work and persistence are key elements of dependable behavior. Remember that it takes time for these qualities to grow. Kids need practice so they can build dependable habits, learn from mistakes, and develop a sense of ownership that lets them acknowledge, "Yes, I can be dependable." If your child is juggling many responsibilities, take the time to talk them through. Your child might need some specific help or just may need to vent.

Enlarge Their Possibility

As they grow, children start to grasp that people depend on them beyond themselves, they may have their family, school, community.

Increasingly, they can be asked to take responsibility for others in the family–which may mean walking a younger child to her classroom or babysitting younger siblings when they're mature enough. Make sure your child is taking their responsibility seriously and stress your pride in seeing them follow through.

Cope with Irresponsible Behavior

Not being dependable often brings natural consequences—for example, skipping doing your homework to hang out with friend's results in lower grades, not showing up for work on time may cost you your employment, and so on. In such cases, don't bail kids out of their lack of being dependable –insist they make good on the homework and apologize to their boss for being late. Focus on how they can do better next time. If they've broken a rule, tell them, "We need to find a way for you to earn back our trust." Link privileges to dependability. For example, if a child wants to go to the mall with friends, he or she needs to finish chores first.

Prepare Them for Independence

One of our most important jobs as parents is to prepare our children to cope with life outside the home. Teach your child basic life skills, such as grocery shopping, cooking, budgeting, doing laundry, and other household tasks. Start an allowance and help your child budget and save for special items. Allow kids to set their own goals and to take the reins as much as they can. Look for ways to let your kids know that you find them trustworthy.

Conclusion

As Parents we must remember that being dependable is an important part of mature behavior. Give kids experience in decision-making early

CHAPTER 2

FEBRUARY

We never know the love of a parent till we become parents ourselves. – Henry Ward Beecher

February is known as the month of love, it is the time when we celebrate Valentine's Day and we make time for remembering our sweethearts. As parents we need to emphasize the importance of having someone special in our lives aka our children and how they make everything in our lives so much better. February is also the month for Random Acts of Kindness, a movement which encourages doing something for other people, randomly, and making their winter more bearable. The concepts for raising extraordinary kids reflect the values of this month. In February, we will have our children volunteer, embrace love and not worry about failure. As parents this month we will boosts faith in good deeds, in being humane, helpful and thoughtful.

Have your children volunteer

A Volunteer is defined as someone who gives time, effort and talent to a need or cause without profiting monetarily. From my personal experience being a volunteer is one of the most rewarding acts that person can engage in. The good news is that volunteering is something that can be shared activity with your children. In fact, children who volunteer have core values reinforced and so much more good stuff also could occur such as:

Helping kids learn

According to the University of Minnesota Youth Development Study, volunteering promotes higher grade point averages and academic confidence. "Service learning" takes this connection a step further to influence not just academic performance but deeper critical thinking, problem-solving skills and the ability to apply what was learned to new situations.

Service learning encourages kids to participate in community service activities that are linked directly to academic topics. For example, 2nd graders can develop reading skills by reading aloud to nursing home residents. Middle- or high-school science students might organize, execute, document and present the results of a water conservation project the city council. There are limitless ways to have our children both gain educational experience and volunteer at the same time. As parents we need sit down with our children and come up with volunteer actives they will enjoy doing and then make contact with different organizations.

Developing real leadership skills

According to leadership expert Karin Hurt, by breaking down hierarchies, group volunteering allows individuals to discover their natural leadership abilities. For kids, group volunteering outside of the classroom lessens the impact that age differences, gender assumptions and social hierarchies have on their ability to find their own leadership voice.

Promotes teamwork and cooperation

There's a reason an increasing number of corporations encourage team-based community service. Group volunteering builds teamwork work relationships by strengthening. When kid participate in community service projects they are aligned under a common goal, leveling distinctions between age, academic performance and social status. This level playing field is also an ideal environment for developing leadership.

Builds empathy

We all value compassion and want our children to nurture this quality in them. But it's not always easy for parents to "teach" compassion on a moment-to-moment basis. Volunteering can

Help. Volunteering helps kids understand how others live, a skill that can build their sense of empathy. Thinking about others puts their own challenges in perspective. Empathy is much more than a philosophical ideal. It can have a profound impact on the way kids experience their lives.

Kids are more likely to feel empathy for people whose experiences they can relate to. The more parents can personalize stories of hardship and tragedy that might otherwise seem like newspaper headlines, the more compassionately kids will respond. Kids may even feel an urgency to put their feelings into action, presenting parents with an opportune moment to help them seek out related volunteer activities.

Spending time with family

Families are busier than ever, but they still want to carve out time to be together. Volunteering is a great way to strengthen family bonds, all while making a difference in the community. Ask your children about what causes are important to them. Encourage your family to learn more about the cause. Families who talk about compassion and service will help children understand why the work they're doing is important to others. Additionally, having a conversation about volunteerism will help ensure the children are prepared for and engaged in the experience.

Volunteering as a family is also an excellent way to close the gap between ages, interests, and more. It's an activity that everyone can enjoy, while learning the value of doing good things for the causes and the people we care about.

How to get started:

The first thing to consider when starting your family volunteer adventure is whether this will be a one-time project or something ongoing. Does your family have the time and desire to commit to a regular schedule of volunteering (every week, once a month, etc.), or do you want to simply choose your opportunities as they come up.

The second factors you and your family want to take into consideration are who should be the beneficiary of your volunteerism. Whatever you choose, make sure it's something your family will enjoy doing. Also remember that your family doesn't have to start big when considering volunteering. Volunteering to help a neighbor; a family member; giving our time to school activities; and even simply helping someone at random are already good but simple acts of volunteering.

Once you decide as a family what to pursue, lay out clear expectations for the experience and do so enthusiastically. Children often mirror their parents' reactions, so it's important that you're excited and pumped for the chance to give back.

Conclusion:

Volunteering can show children just how powerful they are. Your children will see firsthand just how their mere presence can lift the moods of a person in need, for instance, or how excited animals at the rescue center get to be played with. So let's help our kids become extraordinary by teaching them to volunteer.

Teach your Kids to Embrace Love

One of the most important things a parent can teach their child is being able to love another person. We, as parents must teach our children that showing our love and affection to someone is a beautiful thing. Always remember that the best way for kids to learn to embrace love is to see their parents being role models and doing so in everyday life. Here are three ways that we as parents can insure that our children know how to welcome love in their life.

Open Your Kids Eyes

Our kids need to realize that there is so much love right in front of them. Many of them spend the day with their heads buried in cellphones and video games. We must teach our kids to take time to look-up and see just how many people in everyday life care about them. Our children need take the time to really pay attention and listen to family, friends and teachers compliments. Our children must not be afraid to connect with others and to see the goodness that is right in front of them.

Teach Empathy

It's easy for our kids to get caught up in their own daily stresses. But we need to teach our kids to take the time to contemplate the world around them and try to understand someone else's struggle, hope, worry or fear. When our kids learn to listen, offer comfort and understanding to their fellow human being then the power of love can truly be felt.

Emanate Joy

It's an obvious fact: People gravitate towards good energy. What you put out there in the universe is often what you will get in return. So we must raise kids that smile and laugh and are joyful. We must have children who people enjoy having around. Embracing love is one way to insure this occurs.

Conclusion

Remember the most important love to embrace is that between a parent and a child. This love characterized by warmth, affection, care, comfort, concern, nurture, support, acceptance. The parents' love can be felt when they kiss, hug, praise, compliment, or say nice things to or about their children so be sure to show love to your child as often as possible.

Don't Worry About Failure

The final concept for the month of February is to teach our children to not worry about failure. It's sad to say but for many kids the fear of failure can be crippling and make them give up even before they try something new. According to Child phycologist, Dr. Jason Peterman, the fear of failure among children in America today is at epidemic proportions. The fear of failure causes children to experience debilitating anxiety before they take a test, compete in a sport, or perform in a recital. The fear of failure causes our children to give less than their best effort, not take risks, and, ultimately, never achieve complete success.

The Value of Failure

We must teach or children that failure is an inevitable-and essential-part of life. Failure must be taught as something that can bolster the motivation to overcome the obstacles we as humans face every day. Failure can also be a valuable learning tool by connecting children's actions with consequences, which can help them gain ownership of their efforts. According to children's psychologist, Dr. Kenneth Silvestri, failure teaches important life skills, such as commitment, patience, determination, decision making, and problem solving. Failures can also help children respond positively to the frustration and disappointment that they will often experience as they pursue their goals. Failure teaches children humility and appreciation for the opportunities that they're given.

Have Conversations about Success and Failure

As parents the first step in teaching our children to deal with failure is to make sure we are having conversations about the topic. Now when kids are smaller this conversation can be very simple and should focus on trying and how it is ok to fail. Once children are in second grade or older then the conversation can get more complex and then it is encouraged to use example from your own life or from famous people such as Abe Lincoln who lost many local elections before becoming president or Michael Jordan who did not make his varsity basketball team as a sophomore. Remember to explain that failure can be beneficial because it leads to success (when we learn from it and try again). Your child should know that when you fail, you learn about what works and what doesn't, you improve, and you learn to keep going instead of giving up.

Parents must lead by example:

One of the main themes of raising extraordinary kids is to be role models, so we as parents must always remember that children learn from our example. Stanford University researchers Carol Dweck and Kyla Haimovitz have found that kids learn their attitudes about failure from their parents. By watching their parents, children develop one of two ideas: that failure is "enhancing" or that failure is "debilitating." When we as parents fail try to respond with positivity or humor. Be sure that you talk to your child about what you've learned from your mistakes (whether past or present), and how you picked yourself up and tried again.

Emphasize Effort, Not Ability

When children are trying anything new we must first and foremost emphasize giving 100 percent effort. History is full example of people having tons of ability and ending up wasting it or losing out to people who give more effort. Demonstrate that performance is not about ability. It's about effort, practice, learning strategies, and determination.

Carol Dweck of Stanford University and her colleagues studied hundreds of 5th grade children, praising one group for their *abilities* and the other for their *efforts*. Both groups were challenged with a difficult test designed for 8th grade students. The group who was praised for their effort tried very hard, although they naturally made plenty of mistakes. The group who was praised for intelligence became discouraged when they made mistakes, seeing these errors as a lack of ability and a sign of failure. Overall, intelligence testing for the "effort "group increased by 30%, while it decreased by 20% for the "ability" group, all because of different attitudes about mistakes and failure.

This doesn't mean you should simply tell your child, "Try harder," when they struggle (especially if they have truly made an effort). But you can discuss specific strategies that might work next time, rather than saying something ability-oriented like, "its okay if you aren't strong enough to play football."

Help kids focus on the Solution

Instead of telling your son to give up on football because he is not strong enough, as a parent you need to help your kid focus on a solution to get better. The first step is discussing what went wrong or why did your kid fail. The second step to help kids focus on the solution is to find out how to fix or prevent what went wrong for the next time. Make sure that you let your child brainstorm solutions, but you can also make suggestions, such as, "Do you think it would help to join a gym and start lifting weights to get stronger for football?

By helping your kids focus on the solution you're teaching your child not to respond to failures with frustration, disappointment, or giving up. They will learn that failure simply means going back to the drawing board and devising new, better approaches and strategies.

Demonstrate Unconditional Love

According to UC Berkeley professor Matt Covington, the fear of failure is directly linked to your self-worth, or to the belief that you are valuable as a person. Kids usually tie their self-worth to what their parents think about them. They might feel their parents won't love or appreciate them as much if they don't maintain high grades, superb athletic or artistic performance, perfect behavior, etc. Naturally, this belief results in a fear of failure.

As parents it's a given that we love our children unconditionally but be sure to tell them that. Our children need to know that even if they make mistakes or fail at something we love them no matter what the results are. Also be sure that your children know they don't have to be perfect at everything, its ok to get a few answers wrong on a math test or strike out in baseball.

Conclusion

Parents let's make our kids extraordinary by making sure they are able to accept failure. Remember to explain that you will *always* love your children and that you are proud of their effort, persistence, and continued improvement. Of course also remember there is such a thing as, too much failure and that kids should not just go through the motions during activities. Kids need to have some success in order to bolster motivation, build confidence, reinforce effort, and increase enjoyment. As children pursue their life goals, they must experience a healthy balance of success and failure to gain the most from their efforts.

CHAPTER 3

MARCH

"Tell me and I forget, teach me and I may remember, involve me and I learn." – Benjamin Franklin

The month of March brings with it the promise of warm(er), sunny days, as Earth turns its frostbitten cheek to winter and springs forward. With the warmer weather it's a great time to teach our kids how to be stewards of the environment. Now is the time to have our kids help out with some spring cleaning and do chores. Also, this month as parents we will show our kids how it is very important to act locally and support the community we live in.

Be Stewards of the Environment

With 7.5 billion people calling Earth home, creating a cleaner, more sustainable environment probably seems like a daunting task, but what happens if we start by working on ourselves and our children. Your positive environmental impact, while seemingly small in scale, would be the first step to fostering better habits and, in turn, building a clean world we all deserve.

Parents play a valuable role in saving our earth's natural resources and that starts by teaching our children to be stewards of the environment.

The good news is that environmental stewardships can be ridiculously easy, and oftentimes involves small lifestyle adjustments that can yield big results. Here are a few simple tips that you and your child can follow which will have enormous effects on the environment.

Use less Bottled Water

Right now, our planet is consuming one million plastic bottles a minute, with only nine percent of those bottles ever getting recycled (Knott, 2020). In addition to leftover plastic being wasted, significant amounts of oil, energy, and resources, not to mention the emissions of transporting those bottles of water – help contribute to the pollution of our world and neighborhoods as well.

Breaking the convenience of a bottled water habit can be a challenge, but it can be done! A great start is to make a one-time investment in a filtered water pitcher or reusable water bottle, letting you drink clean, filtered water from the local tap. Additionally, keeping a reusable bottle with you and your kids to the gym, to work, or even while your family is busy at home. A reusable water bottle will keep you and your family hydrated without bottled water's negative impact on the environment. Plus, this new eco-friendly habit will be better on your family budget, too!

Remember to Recycle

Simply teaching our children to recycle is an extremely easy way to help out the environment.

We, as parents are not only talking about paper, cans, and bottles here. You should also consider recycling batteries, glass, and used technology. Be sure to familiarize your children with what can and can't be recycled, and what goes where. Also be sure to find your local recycling centers to easily dispose of recyclable items that don't belong in your curbside bin.

Buy Local Food / Grow Your Own

Whether it's from a local farmers market or a community-supported agriculture program, getting food that's grown close to home cuts back on transportation emissions and other effects that often come from delivering food from across the country. In fact, semi-trucks like those bringing blueberries, bananas or watermelon from other parts of the country to your local grocery store account for 11% of carbon emissions. (Texas commission on the Environment, 2019)

If locally-sourced food is hard to come by, consider working with your neighbors to start a community garden. This is a great way to extend your environmental stewardship and train others to do better for the world.

Start Composting

According to the EPA, Americans produce nearly 60 billion pounds of food scraps each year. To stop all that stuff from ending up in landfills, your family should consider cultivating compost instead. Compost and compost products are beneficial to the soil we grow our food in, reduce the need for chemical fertilizers, and reduce methane emissions from landfills, all of which helps to reduce your family's carbon footprint. It's a win-win for the environment, your community, and your family's backyard garden.

You can compost most organic materials, ranging from fruits and vegetables to coffee grounds and tea bags, and to anything yard-related like grass clippings and leaves.

To get started, all you need are three things: some brown organic material, some green organic material, and water. Mix dead leaves, branches, or twigs with grass clippings, vegetable scraps, or fruit peels. Then add water. Composting is very simple and fun way to get the kids involved in becoming stewards of our great planet.

Conclusion

A big movement begins with just one person making a difference. We as parents must be stewards of the environment and pass our love for a clean, beautiful earth to our children. Like everything in life, parents must be good role models so that generations have a clean earth they can be proud of.

Act Locally

As parents if we have shopping to do, it's tempting to take the easy route and head down to the mall – or easier still, just browse Amazon. Major chain stores and Internet retailers offer a vast selection plus the convenience of one-stop shopping. On top of that, their prices often beat the local stores. However we as parents must acknowledge that keeping your dollars in your hometown has other advantages that can be more important than saving a few bucks, even if they're not immediately apparent. By shopping locally, your family reaps such benefits as:

- *A Stronger Economy.* Local businesses hire local workers. In addition to staff for the stores, they hire local architects and contractors for building and remodeling, local accountants and insurance brokers to help them run the business, and local ad agencies to promote it. They're also more likely than chain stores to carry goods that are locally produced, according to the American Independent Business Alliance. All these factors together create a "multiplier effect," meaning that each dollar spent in a local store brings as much as $4.50 into the local economy according to a study done by the chamber of commerce (2019). By contrast, large chain stores tend to displace as many local jobs as they create because they often drive local retailers out of business according to a northwestern study done on economic impact of chain stored in 2017.

- *A Closer Community.* Shopping at local businesses gives neighbors a chance to connect. It's easier to get to know someone you often see at a local coffeehouse than someone you only wave to on your way in and out of your house. Knowing your neighbors makes it possible to have a world with more harmony and love.
- *A Cleaner Environment.* Having stores in your immediate neighborhood means you can leave your car parked and do your errands on foot or by bicycle. Fewer cars on the road means less traffic, less noise, and less pollution. If you made just one trip each week on foot instead of making a 10-mile round trip by car, you would reduce your annual driving by 520 miles. (Cleaner America study, 2018) That would save about 24 gallons of gas and keep 0.2 metric tons of carbon dioxide out of the atmosphere, according to calculations from the Environmental Protection Agency.
- *A Great Place to Live.* The last factor is more difficult to measure than the others, but it's just as important. Local businesses make your town a better, more interesting place to live. One suburban housing development looks much like another, but a town center with thriving local businesses has a feel that's all its own. Local eateries, bars, bookstores, food markets, pharmacies, and gift shops all combine to give a place its unique character.

How to Support Your Local Economy

There are many ways you and your kids can support businesses in your neighborhood. For instance, if you have a local hardware store, look there first when you need anything for your house instead of heading down to the big-box home-improvement store. Most towns have at least a couple of local restaurants or bars, and choosing these places when you eat out is another way to support your local economy. Or buy your produce from a local farmers market or shop for clothes at a local boutique.

Of course, all this depends on exactly which local businesses are available in your town. Since each town's local economy is unique, the first step is learning what businesses you have around you, where they are, and when they're open.

Learn About Local Businesses

To learn more about local businesses in your area, set aside a day to explore your town and see what it has to offer. Since part of the benefit of shopping local comes from being able to run errands on foot, if possible, leave your car at home and focus on the area within walking distance. You may be surprised what unique businesses exist right under your family's nose.

Make local a routine

Once you've identified local businesses in your area, the next step is to make shopping at them part of your usual routine. Since local businesses often can't match the low prices of big-box stores, it's challenging if you're on a tight budget but try to at least find one item to buy local.

Eat Locally

Not all local businesses are useful to everyone. For instance, a pet grooming store isn't of much use to you if you don't have pets. However, everybody has to eat, so shopping locally for food is one of the best ways to support your local economy.

Also buying your food at locally owned grocery stores is a good place to start, but a farmers market is even better. Shopping there gives you a chance to meet not just the people who sell your food, but the people who grow it. The U.S. Department of Agriculture reports that the number of farmers markets in the country has increased nearly fivefold since 1994, so your chances of finding a market in your area are better than ever.

Doing your shopping at farmers markets has several advantages over supermarket shopping:

- *Quality* - Farmers market produce is usually fresher than the goods sold at supermarkets. Since farmers grow the food locally, it hasn't spent days or weeks traveling across the country. The fresher fruits and vegetables are, the better they taste, the more nutrients they retain, and the longer they stay fresh before you eat them.

- *Sustainability* - Locally grown food doesn't have to be shipped long distances, which reduces its carbon footprint – the amount of greenhouse gas produced in growing, harvesting, and transporting it. Also, most sellers at farmers markets are small-scale growers who can more easily adopt green growing practices. According to the Farmers Market Coalition, nearly half of all farmers markets sell organic products – and 3 out of 4 farmers who sell their goods at farmers markets grow food in a way that meets organic standards, even if they don't have official organic certifications. Also, 48% of them use integrated pest management – a method of controlling pests with minimal damage to the environment – and 81% use soil health practices, such as growing cover crops and producing their own compost.

- *Information* - Buying directly from the grower is the surest way to know where your food comes from and how it was produced. At a farmers market, the person behind the counter knows the answer to all kinds of questions a clerk at a supermarket doesn't. For example, they can explain which varieties of apples are better for cooking and which are better for eating or tell you which breed of chicken produced the eggs you're buying and how they raised the hens.

- *Atmosphere* - Farmers markets are typically friendlier, more personal settings than big supermarkets. It's much easier to strike up a conversation with a fellow shopper searching through a bin of melons at the farmers market than with a stranger pushing a cart past you at the grocery store. The Farmers Market Coalition also reports that in a 2018 survey, farmers market shoppers said they typically had 15 to 20 social interactions during each visit as compared to just one or two when they shopped at the supermarket.

A final way to shop locally for your groceries is through a food co-op. A co-op is a grocery store that's owned jointly by the people who shop there, so joining one gives you a say in what the store sells and how it's run. Joining a co-op and attending its meetings is a way to meet and interact with your neighbors. And since most co-ops specialize in food that's locally produced, including organic foods, it's a way to support local growers.

Bank Locally

Another way to keep your money in your community is to literally keep your money at a local community bank or credit union rather than a large national bank. Banking locally offers several benefits:

- *Lower Cost* - Many locally owned banks and credit unions offer the same services as the big national banks, such as credit cards and online bill payment. However, their rates and fees are typically quite a bit better. The National Credit Union Administration, the federal agency that regulates federal credit unions, reports that compared to banks, credit unions usually offer higher interest rates on deposits, lower interest rates on loans, and lower fees. Furthermore, according to the 2019 Banking Landscape Report from Wallethub, checking accounts from community banks are 48% cheaper than those from national banks, pay 45% more interest, and have more features.
- *Better Service* - Community banks and credit unions offer more personal service because they serve a much smaller area.

At a community bank or credit union, the teller will often recognize you, remember your name, and take time to answer your questions. Community banks and credit unions don't always offer the 24-hour phone service you get from the big banks. But anyone who's ever spent time trying to navigate the menu on a national bank's phone lines and connect to a human being knows that isn't much of a drawback.

- *Supporting the Local Economy* - Community banks and credit unions make most of their money from loans to local people and businesses. The Institute for Local Self-Reliance, a community development organization, reports that more than half of all loans to small businesses come from small to mid-size banks and credit unions. Because small local banks make most of their loans within the community, they have an interest in helping that community prosper.

Conclusion

When you teach your kids to invest money in your local economy, they will not be just helping homegrown business owners – they will also helping themselves and their family. Your children will be making their town a better place to live in, with a rich character, thriving economy, and tightly knit community. Also keep in mind that the more local businesses prosper, the more new ones will open, making it even easier to continue shopping locally. Who knows maybe in the future your extraordinary kids will be local business owners.

Have kids do chores

Recently I was having discussion with a mom who said she doesn't make her kids do any kind of house work because she didn't want to "ruin their childhood". This mom was way off base and in fact having children do chores not only immensely benefit the kids but also society. So in order for our kids to be extraordinary our kids need to do chores.

According to a 2019 UCLA study 68% of college freshman on their campus did not know how to do their own Landry and 83% said they could not cook a meal from scratch, one of the reasons for this is the lack of life skills taught to them. These life skills that could easily been learned by parents having their kids do chores. Remember that our kids are young now, but they won't be forever! Laundry, cooking and cleaning are just some of the skills your kids will need once they finally move out. These are also skills that schools do not fully teach anymore like they use to 30 years ago. So parents need to step up. We as parents need to make sure we teach our kids to be both self-reliant and responsible.

Chores that personally affect your kids, such as cleaning their room or doing their own laundry, can help them become more independent. One of the biggest values of kids doing Chores is how it can help build a strong work ethic that can last a lifetime. A strong work ethic is a trait that is valued by teachers and bosses, so why not instill this characteristic in your kids from a young age. Here are a few ideas on how to add chores into your child's life.

Assigning Chores

As a parent you must make sure you assign chores that are age appropriate for each one of your children. Also be sure to choose tasks you need help with not just busy work to get the kids out of your hair for a few hours. Make sure to also take into consideration the life skills your children needs to learn, along with your child's interests and abilities. When assigning chores be sure to ask your children for their input. Remember that children are more cooperative when they have a say in the chores they are assigned to.

Being a role model

The common theme throughout this book is that parents must always be a role model for their children; this is no different when it comes to chores. Remember that in addition to being steadfast in the belief that it is important to have children complete chores, your attitudes can help set the tone that will increase possible cooperation in your household. Parents must be sure to Encourage, praise, show affection and love when your children put in effort. Be patient, do not nag and accept that it will take time to start a child on everyday responsibilities.

Conclusion

Having kids take out the garbage, mow the lawn, and do the dishes are not just ways to make your life easier, they're also a ways to make your kids' lives better, too. The chores that your children are participating in today nurture responsible, independent, and caring adults of tomorrow.

Chapter 4

APRIL

"Being a Parent is learning about strengths you didn't know you had, and dealing with fears you didn't know existed." – Linda Wooten

By April, spring has finally sprung, and if we're lucky, the weather will reflect that! I hope that your sky is bright and clear and your grass is growing green. This is a wonderful time to plant a garden with your kids. This month we will teach our kids to be good listener and the importance of being an organ donor.

Plant a Garden

This month's suggestion comes from one of my own family traditions that go back generations. Each spring my family plants a Garden. This is one of my kid's all-time favorite activities which so far at every age can really appreciate. Remember that planting a garden can have huge benefits for your children other than just having fresh tomatoes and cucumbers. There are also many life lessons that can be learned though planting a garden such as the following:

Teaches Responsibility

Gardening is a great way to teach kids about responsibility. Kids learn that they have to take care of their seeds each day in order for them to become healthy plants. To help, I give each kid a job that last usually a week or two. Some of the jobs would be for example watering, and weeding.

Promotes healthy eating

Every farmer knows that half the fun of gardening is getting to eat what you grow. A study by the department of agriculture (2018) found that students involved in hands-on school gardening programs developed an increased snacking preference for fruits and vegetables. The research supporting this type of gardening program continues to rack up.

When parents get involved in gardening with their kids, the results are even better! The University of Wisconsin- Madison 15 year study on families and growing their own food found a correlation between growing food and increased food preparation at home. The study also found a 40 percent increase in consumption of fresh produce in children that had gardens at home. So grab a shovel with your child and watch the health of your whole family blossom.

Teaches the Ability to Plan and Organize

For those that garden regularly, you understand that planning and organizing a garden can be the biggest factor in success or failure. A good gardener need to know how long it takes a seed to actually turn into a vegetable and when are the best time to plant your seeds are, also how much space is needed for each plant. Involving kids in this process helps increase their planning and problem solving skills. It also enhances their organizational strategies which can be carried over to every facet of life!

Teaches Patience

Over the years the best lesson that my kids have learned from a garden is patience. Most kids in this day and age are used to immediate gratification; however, gardening is often a slow process. Kids have to learn to be patient when waiting for their flowers and vegetables to grow. The waiting actually makes the moment the flower or vegetable sprouts even more thrilling.

Conclusion:

Gardens can be a great place to cultivate a meaningful and fun learning experience for your kids. Gardening offer children an opportunity to learn the life cycle process, by which plants are grown, as well as responsibility, caretaking, independence, and environmental awareness, all lessons which will help your kids to become extraordinary.

Be Good Listeners

Attention all parents; we need to recognize that good listening skills are essential to learning. In fact, according to James Oakland a Children Development specialist at the University of Washington, children who listen well not only develop strong language abilities, they find gaining knowledge in any subject easier, less stressful and more successful. After all attentive listeners retain most of what they hear in the classroom which translated to less time studying and better grades.

The typical baby is a born listener. In fact, according to Dr. Graham from Mayo Clinic, newborn baby's auditory system is the most strongly developed of all the sensory systems. Hearing may be slightly impeded by fluid in the baby's inner ear, but in baby's eagerness to engage they will work around that. Infants tune in to their parents' voices from the womb and are highly motivated to continue doing so. Their survival depends on the ability to listen and learn to communicate needs. The big question is what happens between birth and going to school. The answer is unclear, but here are some ways parents can ensure the development of amazing listening skills for their extraordinary kids.

Remove or avoid distractions.

When we teach our kids to be good listens we must teach them to take a moment to anticipate possible distractions and remove them. Our kids need to make sure their cell phones are turned off first and foremost, also they need to make sure that TV, radio, or any other device that could be distracting are off.

If your child is in a social setting, and they are speaking one-on-one with someone, teach them to try to step aside to a quiet space where they won't be pulled away or interrupted by other people. Definitely teach them not to look over the other person's shoulder while they're talking to see who else is in the room.

Notice non-verbal communication and tone of voice.

According to Dr M. L. Banks, the communications director of Harvard University, hearing someone's words is just a small part of being a good listener. We communicate far more through our expressions, body language, and tone of voice.

When you are listening to someone, also watch them carefully. Some examples of what to be aware of are as followed:

- Are their arms crossed defensively, or are they sitting in an open, confident manner?
- Are they saying, "Everything's fine" with their words, but their face looks pinched and anxious?

Also, listen to how they present what they have to say.

- Do they sound tired, depressed, enthusiastic, confused?
- Are they mumbling, talking too loudly, or stating everything as though it were a question?

As a listener we need to also make sure the following cues occur:

- Nod in agreement to show you are engaged and listening.
- Lean forward toward the other person.
- Smile or show concern appropriately.
- Offer words of affirmation and kindness.
- Give a hand squeeze or a warm touch on the shoulder to show empathy.

These subtle communications speak volumes about your level of engagement, understanding, and interest.

Don't interrupt or change the subject.

If you want your kids to be a good listener, make sure to teach them to allow the speaker to complete a thought without interrupting them.

You've probably encountered people who frequently interrupt, take over the conversation, and use the audience as a platform for talking about themselves or sharing their knowledge or expertise and you probably found it very annoying. Let's raise extraordinary kids not annoying ones, there are already enough of them around.

Conclusion

Becoming a good listener is a skill that needs to be learned and must be practiced. It's far too easy to spin off into your own world of distractions, ideas, and words. As our kids become more skilled at listening, they will find people gravitate toward them more. We as parents will be making sure our kids have a skill that gives them the edge in their future careers and in all of their future relationships.

Become an organ donor

April is National Donate Life month. According to the HRSA over 40,000 people began new lives thanks to organ transplants. As parents we need to teach our kids the importance of being an organ donor. The fact is now more than ever are nation needs organ donors.

About 50 percent of the population is registered organ, eye and tissue donors. If you are not registered yet here are some reasons you and your family should consider getting registered.

You can save or improve people's lives

Donors can give their kidneys, pancreas, liver, lungs, heart, and intestines and save as many as eight people's lives. Eye, cornea, and tissue donations can improve the lives of dozens of people. Eyes can be transplanted to help a blind person see again; skin can be transplanted to help someone with severe burns; tendons can be transplanted to help a person's mobility; and more.

Your donation can help a person who lives in your area – maybe even someone you know

In most instances, your organ donation stays local. Transplant centers work to provide organs to people based on general criteria. This includes:

- How well you match with the donor's blood and tissue type,
- How long you've been on the waiting list and what your medical condition is,
- And how close you live to the person donating

The country is divided into 11 geographic regions, and except for perfect kidney matches or very sick patients who need livers, local recipients take first priority. Seventy-five percent of organs go to local people.

Each of the 11 regions is a part of The United Network for Organ Sharing (UNOS). UNOS is a private, non-profit organization that manages the national transplant waiting list.

One organ donor can help multiple people.

One organ donor has the potential to save eight lives, improve as many as 60 lives and enhance the eyesight of two according to the HRSA.

People are dying while waiting for an organ.

According to donate for life, approximately 22 people die each day or 8,000 a year while they are waiting for an organ match to undergo a transplant.

Organ donation can be a rewarding and positive experience.

It can help a family work through the grieving process and deal with their loss by knowing their loved one is helping save the lives of others.

Conclusion

Please, all parents talk to your children at the right age about how important and easy it is to become an organ donor.

If you're 18 years of age or older, you can sign up with your state's organ and tissue donor registry. See where you can sign up. People under the age of 18 can donate too if they have their parents' permission. Additionally, you can register at your Department of Motor Vehicle (DMV) when you get or renew your driver's license.

At the time you register, you can designate specific organs or tissue you want to donate, if you don't want to donate everything. After signing up, you can remove your name from the registry at any time. So parents, please teach your children how they can become extraordinary by saving the lives of others through organ donation.

CHAPTER 5

MAY

"We cannot always build the future for our youth, but we can build our youth for the future" – Franklin D. Roosevelt

This chapter celebrates the gorgeous month of May! The Sun is warming, the birds are chirping, the flowers are blooming, and hopefully the garden you planted with your kiddos is growing. This is the time of year to teach your kids how to be more adventurous. With all the fresh air your kids should now be getting this month it's also very important to make sure they are getting the right amount of sleep. Now is also the perfect time of the year to put always some of the inside toys and video game systems and enjoy the sunshine.

Be Adventurous

Kids need adventure. It is, in fact, fundamental to their development. It's not that babies and toddlers need to be taken mountain climbing. But they do need to have access to new experiences, due to the fact that your child's brain is forming, growing and changing every minute. Though being adventurous sounds like a simple act, it can pose as a challenge for many parents, who naturally tend to try to keep their kid safe and who step in at the first notice of potential danger or strife. In order for our kids to be extraordinary parents need to pull back and let the adventures start.

According to Dr. Oswald one of the leading experts on human development, "The process of developmentally growing up is all about the pruning that takes place in the brain, and that happens based on experience and reinforcement. So if in an extreme situation, a baby is institutionalized and not allowed to run around, they can never make up for those early years of being held back. It's not just physical restrictions that you see later," says Oswald. In other words, if kids are not allowed to run to the edge every once in a while, that sense of limitation will harm their brain development. So what's a parent to do? Here are five things that parents who want to raise adventurous kids:

Let Kids Explore

Parents who want kids who are confident and unafraid of adventure let their kids explore around the house or at the park. According to Dr. Marshall of Harvard University - children development center, by the time kids are about two years old; they hear the word "no" every seven minutes. Instead of rushing in or limiting a kid's exploration, parents should actively encourage their kids to explore the environment around them, assuming that environment is, of course, baby-proofed. While parents can keep a close eye, they should try not to say "no" as often as they do.

Play Outside more

The bottom line is that most kids' now days really do not play outside enough. The benefits of playing outside are endless and more importantly promotes physical health. Also playing outsides breeds adventure! You can go play in the back yard or at the local park and have a dozen adventures. Go on a bug hunt! Go discover how many different plants you can find. Collect trash to recycle and make it a game.

I guarantee if you let your child have outdoor time every single day, you will see a difference in them. Just watch them as they explore, learn, and have adventures and they will be a much happier child!

Hold Back When kids get minor scrapes

As a Parent I know that it's hard not to rush to our children when they've hurt themselves, but on the playground, a skinned knee is really no big deal. Kids will fall off the jungle gym, trip when running down a hill, and jump off swing sets and sometimes, that will hurt. But parents need to hold back unless a kid is in major physical pain. If a kid falls, parents should wait to see how their kid reacts to the pain. "You'll see this all the time: children will fall down and look over to their parents to see whether they should be upset. And then, if mom is upset, the pain hits," says Dr. Lombardi of the children's institute of Health and Safety. I know it is hard to find that balance of comforting our children to much and too little but we as parents must work to find the "sweet spot" of where our children are learning from being adventures but at the same time not in need of medical attention.

Limit Electronics

Children are quickly losing the ability to be adventurous because so much of their time is spent in front of electronics, dulling their ability to become inspired through books and to play through imagination, like we did as children. One of the most important things we can do for our children is to find that balance of electronic time and outdoors/ imagination time.

Accept All Types of Adventurousness

Not every adventurous kid is going to climb to the top of the jungle gym. For older kids, especially those who are shy, simply meeting a new friend or going to a birthday party where they don't know many people is a type of adventurousness activity that should be celebrated. After all, kids grow into adults, and adults don't spend all of their days on jungle gyms. Giving them the tools to be confident and social with new acquaintances will serve them in the long term just as much as exploring the woods behind your house.

Conclusion

I think adventure beckons in all of us and our children. We as parents need to learn to accept adventures as they come. Remember that raising adventurous kids encourages imagination, bravery, and helps kids (and adults) live life to the fullest.

Allow fewer toys to play with

If your kids are like mine then they have tons of toys but yet it seems to complain that they are bored. I recently came across a study done by the University of Toledo researchers which explains why kids are not being entertained by having a room full of toys. The study hypothesized that "an abundance of toys reduced the quality of children's play, and that fewer toys will actually benefit children in the long-term development."

In the study by the University of Toledo, 36 Children played for half an hour with either four or 16 toys. Kids playing with 16 toys spent less time playing with each toy, moving from toy to toy more frequently. When given only four toys to play with, the toddlers "played with each for twice as long, thinking up more uses for each toy and lengthening and expanding their games, allowing for better focus to explore and play more creatively.

In the book *Clutter Free with Kids*, author Joshua Becker also supports the concept that fewer toys are better for children. Becker echoes the belief that playrooms with fewer toys promote creativity, help develop attention spans and teach kids about taking care of their possessions. "A child will rarely learn to fully appreciate the toy in front of them when there are countless options still remaining on the shelf behind them," (Becker, pg. 143).

Benefits to having fewer toys

Many experts have found that fewer toys benefit your children in the following ways:

- *Kids have better social skills.* Kids learn to develop their relationships, and studies have linked childhood friendships to greater academic and social success during adulthood.
- *Kids learn to take better care of things.* When kids have too many toys, they tend to take care of and value them less since there is always another in the toy bin.
- *Kids spend more time reading, writing, and creating art.* Fewer toys give kids the space to love books and generally discover and develop their talents.
- *Kids become more resourceful.* With only the materials at hand, kids learn to solve problems—a skill with unlimited potential.
- *Kids argue with each other less.* A new toy in a relationship is another reason to establish territory between kids. But kids with fewer toys are compelled to share more, collaborate, and cooperate.
- *Kids learn to persevere.* Kids with too many toys give up too quickly on a toy that challenges them, replacing it instead with another, easier one. In the process, they lose the opportunity to learn patience and determination.
- *Kids become less selfish.* Kids who get everything they want believe they can have everything they want, setting the tone for developing a more unhappy and unhealthy lifestyle.
- *Kids go outside more.* Kids with fewer toys look to the outdoors for entertainment and learn to appreciate nature, so are more likely to exercise, resulting in healthier and happier bodies.

Conclusion

All parents, grandparents, and family friends can make their children more extraordinary by allowing them fewer toys to play with. Remember, the best thing you can give your child instead of a new toy is a personal experience. Children are more grateful when they are able to enjoy an experience with their family members rather than having a material gift. After all a toy may last a few months before it's forgotten about. A personal experience can last a lifetime. So use the money you would spend on an extra toy and take a trip to the zoo or go to a football game instead.

Get more sleep

Children need sleep, plain and simple. We all do. Without enough sleep, we get cranky and, with time, unhealthy. But for children, it's especially important because the effects of sleep deprivation can lead to lifelong problems.

Studies by the University of Michigan have shown that kids not getting enough sleep can contribute to obesity. But even more troubling, studies show that children who don't get enough sleep can end up with behavioral and learning problems that persist for years. Teens that don't get enough sleep are at higher risk for depression and learning problems, and once they are old enough for drivers licenses are more likely to get into car accidents. The bottom line is in order for our kids to be extraordinary they need more sleep.

Here are the recommended amounts of sleep per age group according to the National academy of sleep 2019 study of proper sleep habits:

- Infants: 12 to 16 hours (including naps)
- Toddlers: 11 to 14 hours (including naps)
- Preschoolers: 10 to 13 hours (including naps)
- Grade school-aged children: 9 to 12 hours
- Teens: 8 to 10 hours

Ultimately, though, it's up to us as parents to make sure their child gets enough sleep.

Here are four ways you can help your child get enough sleep:

Make sleep a priority

Parents must be sure to schedule time for sleep just like they do on a regular basis for homework, sports, and other activities. Start from when your child needs to get up in the morning, and then count back the number of hours your child needs to sleep and set a non-negotiable bedtime.

For tweens and teens, this may lead to some tough conversations and decisions about schedules and activities, and may mean cutting back on some activities, finding ways to get homework done earlier, and pushing some leisure activities (like video games) to weekends

Start the bedtime routine earlier.

Remember that it is really hard to go right from a physically or mentally intense activity right to sleep. If bedtime is 8:00 pm, that means that your child needs to start winding down between 7 and 7:30 so that they are ready to actually fall asleep at 8.

Shut off the screens.

A big part of winding down is making sure our kids shut off their screens, The blue light emitted from screens can wake up the brain and make it harder to fall asleep. This is particularly true for "small screens" such as phones or tablets that are held closer to the face. Shut them off an hour before you want your child to be asleep. Phones should be charged outside of the bedroom — or at the very least, put in Do Not Disturb mode. If your child tries to tell you they need their phone to wake them up in the morning, buy them an alarm clock.

Keep the same sleep routines on weekends

Another important way parents can be sure their child gets enough sleep is to try and keep the same sleep routines on the weekends. A little leeway is okay, like staying up an hour or so later if your child can and will sleep later in the morning (if you have one of those kids who is up at dawn no matter what aka my son Jaxson, staying up later may not work out so well).

Remember, the common theme of being a role model throughout this book, and that children pay more attention to what we as parents do than what we say. If you make your own sleep a priority, you will set a good example for your child — and feel better yourself.

Conclusion

Parents remember that sleep is essential for the good health of our children. In fact, just like food and water we need sleep to survive. We as parents need to make sure that our kids are getting enough sleep so they don't experience side effects such as poor memory and focus, weakened immunity, and mood swings. Let's not overlook something that affects 1/3rd of our child's life and make sure they are getting enough sleep daily.

CHAPTER 6

JUNE

"I became the kind of parent my mother was to me." – Maya Angelou, poet

The month of June brings beautiful bouquets of flowers and an urge to get out there and enjoy the sunshine. This month is a nice time to stop at a lemonade stand or grill out and eat meals as a family. It's also the perfect time to start to read to your kids daily, it could be around a camp fire or lying on a beach. The bottom line is you and your kids need to enjoy the beautiful summer weather together.

Stop at lemonade stands

The other day when I was driving to work I saw two little girls with a lemonade stand on the corner. Usually in the summer time there are a bunch of these in my small city and for many years I would drive by these stands with my head down so I don't make eye contact with the sweet kids running them. However for some reason this one time instead of driving by I decided to stop. For the bargain price of 50 cents I bought a cookie and a cup of lemonade. The two kids were so delighted to have a sale that they thanked me five times for stopping. As I drove to work eating my cookie I couldn't help but think about how awesome the pure joy those kids felt just from making a simple 50 cent sale. After that one experience I decided that from this day forward I will now stop at all the lemonade stands that I come across and more importantly once I had kids help them set up lemonade stands.

So as the middle of summer rolls around, I encourage everyone to stop at the next lemonade stand you see. By doing so, not only will you make a child's day but there are also some great life lessons that can be promoted. The idea of being an entrepreneur and the satisfaction of having a small business is one major concept that is being learned by children who run a lemonade stand. Also these young business savvy kids are able to realize the value of earning money through working and providing their neighborhood with a service. This is lost in this day and age where many kids expect everything, including money to be just handed to them. Remember that someday the kids that run these lemonade stands are the future leaders of our community so the least we can do is support their business. So help your community kids become extraordinary and stop at all the lemonade stands you see in the month of June.

Read to your kids daily

The other day I overheard my kids talking about their favorite time of the day and I was shocked to find out that all three agreed it was at night before bed when I would read to them As a dad trying my best to raise extraordinary kids, hearing this made me very happy since many studies done over the last 50 years show that toddlers and preschoolers who are read to every day become successful adults.

It is often recommended that parents spend at least 15 or 20 minutes reading with their kids each day. This minor amount of time out of your day can produce massive advantages that can change your child's life forever. Besides growing up to be extraordinary here are some of the other benefits that your children will get from you reading to them daily.

Developing language skills

Reading books to your children ensures that they are exposed to vocabulary on different topics, which means they hear words or phrases which they may not hear otherwise in their day to day lives. The more words they know the better and the faster they will develop language skills.

Enhances concentration

While most babies and toddlers may have trouble sitting still for everyday actives, reading to your child consistently every day can teach concentration. Just by adding a minutes each month to your story time can insure your child can concentrate better for long periods of time, which can help later on when they go to school.

Encourages a thirst for knowledge

When you read to your child every day, it's a given that questions about the book and the information within will come up. The time you spend reading will gives you a chance to speak about what is happening in the books along with an easy pathway to teach about different subjects.

Development of imagination and creativity

One of the great benefits of reading to your child every day is that their imagination is growing. When we really engage in a book we imagine what the characters are doing. We imagine the setting as reality. Seeing the excitement on a child's eyes when they know what is going to be on the next page, or having them guess what is going to happen is one of the most amazing parts of being a parent.

Books are entertaining

Before there was Netflix's and Facebook and T.V. and radio there were books. Reading can be a great form of entertainment. With all of the negative effects of screen time, choosing a book that interests your child, and either reading it together, or letting them flip through pages alone, is definitely a better option. One of the main benefits of reading to your child every day is that when they are older they will more likely to choose a book to read for pleasure over another activity when they are bored.

Bonding with your child

It is tradition in my house for me to read a book to my kids right before they go to bed and there is nothing I look forward too at night then this chance to bond with my kids. We as parents need to put down the smart phones and turn off our own technology and spend time with our kids. For parents who work, or have a busy lifestyle, relaxing with your child and simply enjoying each other's company while reading can be a great way for you both to wind down, relax, and bond.

Conclusion

The simple activity of reading to your child every night can positively change their life forever. Remember to be consistent, be patient, and don't be selfish take 15 minutes and bond while you read with your child every day.

Eat Meals as a Family

Sadly, Americans rarely eat together anymore. In fact, according to a study by healthykids.gov,the average American eats one in every five meals in their car, one in four Americans eats at least one fast food meal every single day, and over 80 percent of American families report eating a single meal together less than five days a week. It's tragic that so many Americans are missing out on what could be meaningful time with their children the fact is that not eating together also has quantifiably negative effects both physically and psychologically on children.

According to a study by Michael Cambridge (2015), children who do not eat dinner with their parents at least twice a week were 40 percent more likely to be overweight compared to those who do. On the contrary, children who do eat dinner with their parents five or more days a week have less trouble with drugs and alcohol, eat healthier, show better academic performance, and report being closer with their parents than children who eat dinner with their parents less often, according to a study conducted by the National Center on Addiction and Substance Abuse at Columbia University.

The good news is that Children who eat regular family dinners also consume more fruits, vegetables, vitamins and micronutrients, as well as fewer fried foods and soft drinks. And the nutritional benefits keep paying dividends even after kids grow up: young adults who ate regular family meals as teens are less likely to be obese and more likely to eat healthily once they live on their own. Research by USDA (2016) has even found a connection between regular family dinners and the reduction of symptoms in medical disorders, such as asthma. The benefit might be due to two possible byproducts of a shared family meal: lower anxiety and the chance to check in about a child's medication compliance.

It isn't just the presence of healthy foods that leads to all these benefits. The dinner atmosphere is also important. Parents need to be warm and engaged, rather than controlling and restrictive, to encourage healthy eating in their children. When parents have dinner conversation with their children not only will they be healthier and happier but also smarter.

Family meals = smarter kids

Research by Shannon Bream (2017), found that for young children, dinnertime conversation boosts vocabulary even more than being read aloud to. The researchers counted the number of rare words – those not found on a list of 3,000 most common words – which the families used during dinner conversation. Young kids learned 1,000 rare words at the dinner table, compared to only 143 from parents reading storybooks aloud. Kids who have a large vocabulary read earlier and more easily.

A study by the National Association Healthy Children, found that a consistent association between family dinner frequency and academic performance. Adolescents who ate family meals five to seven times a week were twice as likely to get A's in school as those who ate dinner with their families fewer than two times a week.

Conclusion

Remember the real power of dinners lies in their interpersonal quality. If family members sit in stony silence, if parents yell at each other, or scold their kids, family dinner won't have positive benefits. Sharing a healthy dinner won't magically transform parent-child relationships however it could turn into something extraordinary. According to Anne Fishel, author of The Family Dinner Project, diner may be the one time of the day when a parent and child can share a positive experience – a well-cooked meal, a joke, or a story – and these small moments can gain momentum to create stronger connections away from the table.

CHAPTER 7

JULY

"Tell me and I forget, teach me and I may remember, involve me and I learn." – Benjamin Franklin

July is the month when summer has a firm hold on all of us. The average temperature just about everywhere in the United States is above 70°F, and thunderstorms are nearly as abundant as ants at a picnic! This month also has our nation's birthday and fireworks which is the perfect time to teach our kids why America is such a great country. Now is the time to go to an outdoor concert and expose your kids to music. July is also a perfect time to have a garage sale with your children and make a few extra bucks while teach valuable lessons at the same time. So let the month of July be another stepping stone towards your kids becoming extraordinary.

Expose your Kids to Music

According to a study by Dr. James Petit, a great way to make our kids extraordinary is to expose them to music. Listening to music can boost memory and motivation simply by stimulating different regions of the brain. The right kind of music can relieve stress, improve communication and increase a person's efficiency both at work and school. Music can be used as very powerful tool in the development of our kids!

Music and the Brain: The Benefits of Music

A 2016 study at the University of Southern California's Brain and Creativity Institute found that musical experiences in childhood can actually accelerate brain development, particularly in the areas of language acquisition and reading skills. According to the National Association of Music Merchants Foundation (NAMM Foundation), learning to play an instrument can improve mathematical learning and even increase SAT scores.

Academic achievement isn't the only benefit of music education and exposure. Music ignites all areas of child development and skills for school readiness, including intellectual, social-emotional, motor, language, and overall literacy. It helps the body and the mind work together. Exposing children to music during early development helps preschoolers learn the sounds and meanings of words. For children and adults, music helps strengthen memory skills.

Music is a mood lifter

We all have at some point tucked our children in with a lullaby or calm them down with a song. Just as music can soothe a child, it can also lift their spirit. I love to play club music with my kids on the way to school to get them all pumped up and ready to go for the day. Also there is nothing better than listening to a silly song and busting out laughing. Music is a very powerful tool in changing moods and can even be used by us parents to make us have a better day.

Conclusion:

My goal as a dad is to foster a love of music in my children and then sit back and watch as they benefit from increases brainpower and memory, not to mention stoke the fire of creativity. So we as parents need to make our kids extraordinary by encouraging them to listen to music.

Have a Garage sale

A garage sale is a great way to get rid of unwanted stuff and make some extra cash; it is also a great way to teach your kids many life lessons. According to James Elman, the director of the Children's bureau of learning, "Involving your kids in your yard sale is a great way to teach them some very basic business principles that they can build upon their entire lives. As the world favors entrepreneurial skills more and more, such lessons become ever more valuable." Some of the lessons that my three kids learned were as followed:

How to let go

Parting with once loved toys can be difficult for children. Having a garage sale is a great way to teach children of all ages to go through their belongings and determine what they need and what is just taking up space. Have your children make separate piles, one to keep and one to sell. Encourage them to make these choices independently. Doing so will help them learn how to let go of things easier and not grow up to be hoarders with piles of used magazines making mazes throughout their house. NO one wants that!

The value of money

It is never too soon to teach your children the value of a dollar and a garage sale is a perfect opportunity to do this. A garage sale is a great time to teach kids the lesson that once something leaves a store and used it starts to loose significant value aka deprecates. Also kids can learn that the condition of items matter and that something well taken care of stuff holds its value more then something that is broken and missing parts. When preparing for your garage sale is sure to sit down with your kids and price everything. A good rule of thumb is price items at 90 percent of retail. So if they have a Barbie doll that was bought new for $10.00 a fair garage sale price would be $1.00.

Advertising

Another great lesson that your kids can learn from a garage sale is the importance of using advertising to insure people come and buy your junk. Online ads have replaced the newspaper as the number one spot to tell people about your sale. Most people use social media sites like Facebook or selling sites like Craigslist. Also be sure to make signs with your kids and show them that putting them on busy nearby roads is a value advertising tool as well.

Practice handling money

Once the sale starts be sure to have the kids sit by you and watch you make change. If they are old enough and the sale isn't crazy busy let your children practice doing math. Sadly I find many adults have trouble making change without a cash register helping them out so this is a lost skill that all kids need to learn.

Donate

When it's time to close up shop, the last thing you want to do is bring the unsold items back into your home. Research in advance a local charity that will accept the types of items you are selling and with you kids drive over and drop off and be sure they know that by doing this you are helping people in need.

Conclusion:

Having a garage sale is a fantastic way to teach your children many life lessons. From setting up the yard sale to helping customers, all the way through donating the unsold items once the sale is complete. The garage sale will give your children the chance to practice many skills that will help them throughout their life. So all you parents out there let's make our kids extraordinary and have a garage sale!

Teach Your Children why America is great

Patriotism is defined by the Webster dictionary as "the feeling of attachment and commitment to a country, nation, or political community." Our children must learn about patriotism if they are to grow into well-informed, active citizens. In many of schools Social Studies classes have taken a backseat to science, math, and technology classes as the importance of S.T.E.M. (Science, Technology, Engineering, Math) has skyrocketed. It's sad to say that civics classes are largely a thing of the past.

The United States needs a citizenry that understands such patriotic ideals as the rights and responsibilities of citizenship, the meaning of the Pledge of Allegiance, what it means to live in a republic, and the meaning of liberty and justice for all. The responsibility now falls on to parents to teach these important concepts of patriotism to children. Here are some ideas on how to get your children to become more patriotic as they grow:

Teach about our Flag

The next time you're with your child and you see an American flag, point it out. Explain that it stands for our whole country and that it's one way we tell the world who we are as a people. It also shows we're connected to each other as Americans.

At home, look at a flag together and point out that each part has a meaning. The 50 stars stand for our 50 states. The 13 stripes stand for the original 13 British colonies, whose citizens decided in 1776 that they wanted to govern themselves rather than be ruled by a king.

Teach our Pledge

If your child is in school, they may have recited the Pledge of Allegiance, but like many other kids and adults, they might not understand exactly what the words mean.

According to Dr R.M Palmer, director of American Civics, the pledge is simply a promise. We're giving our word that we'll be loyal (allegiance) to our country, which the flag stands for, because it's a place where we can decide who our leaders will be (republic), where everyone sticks together (indivisible), and where our goal is for people to be free (liberty) and treated fairly by others (justice).

Importance of Independence Day

You don't have to wait until the July 4 festivities to explain what the fun is about. Remember that July fourth isn't just about fireworks that it is our country's birthday. It marks the day in 1776 that a group of determined patriots declared our independence – aka that no other country could rule us as Americans.

Importance of Communities

Your child's home and community are the most real and important parts of America to them. "Kids become patriotic gradually as they learn how they fit into their family and how their family fits into their larger community and then their country," says Anne S. Robertson, a spokeswoman for the National Parent Information Network, a nonprofit organization associated with the U.S. Department of Education.

Take a walk together around your neighborhood, and talk about the values shared by the members of your community. Show your child some of the ways in which people work together and depend on each other. Truck drivers, shopkeepers, repair people – along with many others – help keep the community running. "Our nation is built on cooperation," says Michael Berson, Ph.D., an associate professor of social-science education at the University of South Florida, in Tampa. Seeing the community in action reassures and enlightens young children, and it teaches that we're all in this together.

Teach kids to Honor Police and people who protect us

Young kids are comforted by the knowledge that there are people whose job it is to protect and help us. Some, like police officers, crossing guards, and park rangers, work nearby. Others, like the men and women in our army and navy, may work farther away. Your child can feel confident that no matter where these people are, they're ready to keep us safe. A tour of your local fire station can help your child experience this in a real and exciting way.

For older kids, point out that our government is made up of people whose job it is to serve us. These include public-school teachers, postal workers, sanitation workers, our president, and the other people we've picked to make rules for us, whom we call our senators and representatives.

Teach the responsibilities Americans have to their country

We must teach our extraordinary kids how our country is like a family: Everyone needs to pitch in. As a member of our country – a citizen – we go to school, vote, obey the law, and pay taxes. When your child sees you pick up litter off the ground, point out that being a good citizen means more than just following the law. It means doing what you can to help others and to keep your community clean and safe. You can also set an example through community service. Find something that is important to your child, such as helping out at their school or cleaning up a playground, and do it together as a family. Even if you volunteer only two or three times a year, you'll send your child a very positive message about how citizens pitch in.

Conclusion

We as parents are responsible to teach our children the overarching values that can contribute to making our country great throughout the years to come. If children understand the importance of being contributing members of their communities then they will grow up to be active, caring citizens. When our children having a love and respect for American it makes for a stronger, safer place to live.

CHAPTER 8

AUGUST

Children are apt to live up to what you believe of them." – Lady Bird Johnson

August is the month where summer starts to come to the end and our children start getting ready to go back to school. This is a perfect time for parents to take a well-deserved break from their kids so they can "recharge their batteries" before the busy months of the year start which will be full of after school actives and holidays like thanksgiving and Christmas. This is also a good time to start school preparation which should include getting your kids excited about math. This month is also perfect to make sure your kids are aiming for excellence and aren't settling for average.

Give Parents a Break

This month suggestion has to do with the concept of parental burnout. Parental burnout is defined as feeling exhausted, less productive and emotionally withdrawn. Parents need their own downtime and personal lives away from their children. If you are spending all of your free time running your children to their commitments, you're not taking good care of yourself. So let's make our kids extraordinary by giving moms and dads a chance to recharge.

We as a society need to help each other so find a relative, neighbor or friend from work and offer to watch their kids and give them much needed time to themselves away from the kiddos. Giving free time could be as simple as offering to take the neighbors kids to a park for a few hours, which is something I do frequently or it could be something as elaborate as planning a week cruise long cruise with the grandkids. When it comes to being a parent any free times always helps and believe me is always much appreciated.

Parents make sure that if someone proposes to give you a break be sure to take them up on the offer and don't feel guilty for taking time away from your children. It is easy as a parent to become socially isolated from the outside world. Remember that parents who are able to have breaks away from their children are able to recharge their batteries which leads to more focused and successful parents. After all taking care of children takes an enormous amount of energy and can wear out even the best parents.

Get kids excited about math.

Math is not important to just computer visionaries and Nobel Prize winners. For Parents the main reason we need to get our kids excited about math is because it produces adults who can navigate regular daily life with confidence.

Nevertheless, despite all the recent focus on the importance of science, technology, engineering and math (STEM) fields, our schools have made little change in how we teach math or how they instill excitement for the subjects. Most schools still hand out uninspired worksheets as an ineffective alternative to hands-on materials and true exploration, leaving too many students either lost and confused or ahead and bored. That's why parent engagement in their children's math learning is so crucial. According to Dr. James Detmer, when kids encounter math as a list of abstract facts behind the classroom door, they're given little incentive to remember the material or to apply it to everyday life. A recent report shows that the key to boosting math learning is to expand the number of stations available to children, allowing them to immerse themselves. Making math fun can be seen as a challenge. Below are some ideas that will help your child not be bored and at the same time learn:

Make math a game

Who doesn't like to play games? Games are the perfect way for your kids to learn and have fun at the same time. There are a wide variety of game types that you can use when teaching or reviewing math concepts. These can be computer games, card games, or even ones that you as a parent make up.

Encourage math talk and questions

I think all parents would agree that kids when at home like to talk and ask questions, something that might not happen when in a school setting. We as parents must try to have meaningful conversations about math. This could be about why math is important or how you as an adult us math in everyday life.

Implement engaging routines

Sometimes a little repetition is not a bad thing. As a parent, I have noticed one thing to be true is that Kids respond well to routines. Having a math routine will help you maximize time because your kids know the set expectations. As long as you keep the routines engaging, kids will be tuned in and look forward to more math time.

Use online resources

There are so many cool math websites and apps that you can download to review math skills. Some favorites are prodigy, doddlemath, and buzzmath

Get up and move

We know that children and adults have different learning styles, so mix things up a little bit and include activities where students have to get up and move. It can be a brief brain break that includes math or a longer activity that where students must sort themselves into groups. Either way, your kinesthetic learners will thank you.

Conclusion

Parents who guide their children to use math and science regularly also help them develop a fluency that will serve them well as adults. In the future when our children enter into a financial negotiation, make a major purchasing decisions or even buy ice cream they will be confident in there math skills . As a bonus, some of our kids who fall in love with math could become the next visionaries in the field of software design biotech, or many other jobs that will better the quality of life for us all.

Teach kids to Aim for Excellence

Do your children seem contented just coasting through life? Are they doing just enough to get by, while never making the most of their potential? Most parents do not want their children to grow up living in their basement playing video games all day. So it is of the upmost importance we as parents teach our children to see the significance of aiming for excellence.

Just to be clear, aiming for "excellence" is not merely referring to getting straight A's or racking up accomplishments on the basketball court. There's nothing wrong with working towards these kinds of achievements. But the pursuit of excellence is about much more than that. It's about the following:

- Becoming the best that you can be.
- Cultivating a deep love for learning.
- Making a difference in the lives of others.
- Maximizing your talents and abilities.

This section will give you as parent's ways to inspire your children to pursue excellence.

Emphasize contribution over achievement

Many children and teens lose motivation when they feel as though they can't live up to the expectations of those around them. This applies especially in the area of academics, because they feel strong pressure to achieve certain grades. When they don't get those grades, they become discouraged. To enable your children to regain focus and motivation, emphasize that education isn't primarily about getting good grades. Instead, it's about acquiring the skills and knowledge that will allow them to contribute more effectively. By focusing on contribution rather than achievement, your children will find greater purpose in their education. This will make it more likely that they'll pursue excellence.

Show your children that hard work is enjoyable

In order for your children to make the most of their potential, they'll need to put in plenty of hard work. The problem is, most of our children see hard work as something to be avoided whenever possible. But hard work is both meaningful and rewarding. To help your children see this, share with them the joy of overcoming obstacles, solving problems, and reaping the fruit of their labor. Gradually, they'll start to see that hard work isn't something to be dreaded. It's something to be enjoyed!

Give your children descriptive praise

What's descriptive praise? It's the kind of praise where you acknowledge your children's good behavior by specifically describing what they did, rather than using generic phrases like "Well done" or "Good job".

For example, you might say to your children, "I noticed that you finished all your homework before going out with your friends. That's very responsible of you."

Descriptive praise is an effective tool in encouraging your children to improve their attitude and effort which will lead to excellence.

Focus on solutions – not problems

This is especially important when it comes to parents own life, because after all your attitude affects your children's attitude.

So make an effort to reframe problems as opportunities, and explain to your children how you're taking advantage of these opportunities. By doing so, they'll be more likely to embrace this positive mindset too.

In addition, teach your children to ask this question whenever they're faced with a difficult situation: "What is one thing I can do right now to make the situation better?" This is a powerful question that will open their eyes to the productive actions they could take, rather than indulging in complaining.

Conclusion

As a parent, you want your children to maximize their potential, and to find long-term fulfillment and success. In order for this to happen we must do what we can for our kids to aim for excellence. When this occurs our children will be one step closer to be extraordinary.

CHAPTER 9

SEPTEMBER

It's the little things you do day in and day out that count. That's the way you teach your children." – Anonymous

The month of September is when fall starts and summer ends. This is the perfect time to start teaching your kids something new every day. This month also is the time that our kids go back to school and may start fall after school actives, now is the time to have them get involved in sports. Not only is September a good month but EVERY month should be a good time to put away your phone and focus on your kids. So say bye-bye to your phone this month and really emphasis on raising extraordinary kids

Teacher your kids something new everyday

Many scientist believe that the "brain is like a muscle." Just like other muscles, you have to exercise the brain by learning new things. Yes, there is ample research which shows that learning helps build neuron connections and can stave off diseases like Parkinson's. But there is a lot more to learning new things than just making the brain stronger. The act of learning actually makes us happier.

As Belle Beth Cooper writes about in her post on "Why New Things

Make Us Feel So Good", there is a section in the brain known as the SN/VTA.

The SN/VTA part of the brain is linked to the learning and memory parts, but it is best known as the "novelty center" because it lights up when exposed to new stimuli. You experience a rush of dopamine, which is one of the chemicals that motivate us towards rewards.

Here is what happens:

- You experience something new.
- The "novelty center" of your brain is activated. .
- You get a rush of dopamine.
- Dopamine motivates you to follow through with the new thing.
- You get another rush of dopamine when you finish the activity.

It is no surprise then that research has found dopamine is closely linked to the learning process. In short, learning new things stimulates happiness chemicals in your brain. When your kid's brain is happy then they are one step closer to being extraordinary. Here is a step by step way to teach your soon to be extraordinary kids something new every day:

Pick a topic

Since there are literally billions of topics you could teach your children about each day, the first step that needs to be taken is to have some organization and purpose to the daily learning process. For me personally I decided that I would narrow the subjects to three different categories; the first subject would be something that my kids are interested in and enjoy talking about. For my kids they love the zoo and the nature center so the topic will be animals. I decided the second subject would be something that I enjoy which is football, more specifically the Green Bay Packers. The Third subject would be something simple yet something they could use in everyday life which is a new vocabulary word that they can apply in school.

I suggest picking subjects that your kids are fascinated with and that the topic is something that you and your child can bond over. I also suggest teaching your children something that can help them get ahead in school and life as well. It could be a subject that they are currently learning about or even a foreign language. Again, the key is making sure the subject is something that is enjoyable to talk about by both you and your children and that this activity is something that you both look forward to each day.

Time and Place

Once a subject is chosen to be taught to your child the next step is to figure out both a time and place for the learning to take place on a consistent basis. For me, the time and place is when I'm driving my kids to school in the morning. So far my kids and I usually talk about an animal for anywhere from 2 minutes to the whole 15 minute car ride. If the conversation only last for only a few minutes I then move on to the next subject Green Bay Packers Players. Since my kids are younger this conversation doesn't last long and then finally we talk about a new word and what it means and how to use it in the sentence.

Besides the car ride to school other great times and places that could be used to teach your children something new is at the table while eating a meal also bath time or even right before you tuck them in for the night would be great times as well. Ideally use around 5 to 15 minutes to both teach and then allow for discussion. My kids usually have a least one question that they ask about the subject.

If you are unable to see the child in your life on a daily basis a great way to teach them something new each day is through emails or texts. For example each night you could email your grandchild a new type of Shark to learn about each day. Be sure to include pictures and videos attached in the email along with a few sentences about the subject.

Use Technology

We are lucky to live in the technology age, where all the information a parent would ever need is on our phones and computers. Just by doing a simple google search on a subject can bring endless amount of information right in front of us. Be sure to use all the tech resources out there such as YouTube and Wikipedia. Definitely do a web search on the subject you are teaching your children and make sure to use a many pictures and videos as possible. Remember many kids are visual learners so adding any kind of graphic information on your subject is a major plus.

Conclusion

By teaching a child in your life something new every day you are making them extraordinary. Remember learning makes your kids more interesting to their peers and also makes it easier for them to relate to more people. The more they know, the more likely they are to find something in common with others.

Practice makes perfect when it comes to our children and learning. When our children are mastering new knowledge and skills, they build self-efficacy. Empowering is also a byproduct of learning something new every day. Learning gives your kids the information they need to make better informed decisions in life. Finally learning fuels creativity in our children. As Positive Psychology champion Vanessa King says, ideas come from seemingly unrelated things. Learning new things can trigger ideas in other areas.

Put your phone away and focus on your kids

In today's society we see parents on their phones at playgrounds, at restaurants, in cars, seated around dinner tables, at school functions, on vacation—basically everywhere. According to Jenny Radesky from psmagagine.com, when parents' attention is directed at a smartphone, we talk to our children less, miss their bids for attention, overreact to their annoying interruptions, and think less clearly about what their behavior means.

This has become such an issue that some cities have begun public-service campaigns to increase parents' awareness of the toll their heavy technology use may be taking on child development and well-being. A German boy even organized a rally with over 20,000 children to protest modern parents' preoccupation with technology.

There's good reason to want parents to talk, play, and relate to their children more positively and sensitively. Research suggests that a high proportion of child social-emotional and academic success can be attributed to positive parenting and secure attachment. We don't need to be perfect parents, responsive to our children's needs all the time, but we do need to be "good enough," as the pediatrician Donald Winnicott put it. What this approach translates to in practical terms is kids can feel that we're more interested in our phones than we are interested in them.

The good news is that this is a fixable problem. For most people, it's simply a matter of admitting to the issue, and making a simple plan with the rest of the family. Below are some suggestions.

Have family discussion about appropriate cellphone use

The first step for parents to take in order to lose the cellphone is to have discussion about their use with their family. Even young kids can contribute to a conversation about phone use around the house. This will help them understand why you occasionally need to get on the phone. It will also help them understand why you set rules on their technology usage. Ask them what they think appropriate electronic media use looks like and what sorts of consequences might be warranted for breaking the agreed-upon rules. You may have to help guide them in these discussions, but often you'll find that they have expectations that are not that different from your own

Make a list of why you use your phone at home

It's useful to write a list of your important everyday phone activities. This list will be slightly different for every parent. Ask yourself what phone activities are critical for your job vs those that are fun and refreshing? Use this list to make time to check your phone without interrupting family moments. Account for work and play on your phone – you need both. The key is for parents to reassert control over their phone by figuring out how they actually use it.

Consider Your Habit Triggers

In The Power of Habit, Charles Duhigg wrote "Most of the choices we make every day may feel like the products of well-considered decision making, but they're not."

We automatically reach for our phones in certain situations. Try to pay attention to these cues or triggers. When do you automatically reach for your phone? What can you do differently during those times, besides look at your phone? Or how can you change the way you're using your phone in those moments to include your kids. For example if you are watching the highlights from the basketball game the night before have your son sit next to you want watch them with him and then engage in conversation about what you saw.

Make Family rules

Once you have good conversations with your children and figured out the reasons to use / not use your phone at home then rules must be established. Some example of rules that could be made are as followed:

- No phones out for the first hour after coming home
- No phones out until the kids are in bed
- No phones out during meals
- No phones out during a family movie

Parents, make sure you designate a spot or drawer where you will stash your phone during the rules period.

Conclusion

As parents we must take into account that intense attention we devote to our phones has a major, measurable impact on our health, wellbeing, and most importantly our family relationships. We must create healthy phone boundaries. These boundaries should be something that we should all hope our kids might inherit and follow outside of your home, and may even pass down to their own kids someday.

Have your kids play sports

Having your kids participate in sports is another step that we as parents can take to make children extraordinary. Youth sports promote the value and importance physical activities can have on the emotional, bodily, social, and mental development of your children. Here are some other really good reasons why you should sign your child up for sports as soon as possible.

Social Skills

When playing sports kids will communicate and interact with other kids and adults (coaches). One of the most important traits children need to develop is their social skills. The best way to develop your child's social skills is by having them participate in sports. Especially in team sports, kids will have to communicate with coaches and teammates on a regular basis. Parents, the bottom line is if you want your kids to be more social you have to put them in social situations.

Physically Fitness

Childhood obesity is running rampant across our entire country. Obesity is contributed to poor dietary habits and constant inactivity. Playing sports will keep kids physically active. Sports will compel kids to become better athletes because they will be executing a variety of different exercises during practice. They will strengthen their body and the constant exercise will help reduce stress and build their self-esteem. Let's not forget that physical fitness will help develop coordination as well. Kids that play sports will have better balanced, core strength, posture, and overall coordination than a kid that sits and plays video games all day long. When parents allow their children to become obese, they are setting them up for failure.

Keeps Kids Busy

Sports will keep kids busy and around other kids that are on the same path. Participating in sports will put your child in a safe and structured environment. They will be learning a variety of different skills that they will take with them as they grow older. I much rather have my kid come home from school and go to practice, rather than come home and go on YouTube all night long. Also according to the Department of Education, kids that participate in sports on a regular basis are less likely to drop out of school and do drugs.

Develops Competitiveness

Life is full of situations where you have to compete. One of the worst traits you can have is the unwillingness to compete. In today's world if people aren't willing to compete they will find themselves getting the short end of the stick on a regular basis. Being competitive isn't just about being better than everyone else. Kids need to learn to challenge and compete with themselves to become better every day. Every single successful person I know is competitive. They are not just competing with others; they are very driven and are always competing with themselves. When kids grow older they will need to be competitive in school, for jobs, and in all aspects of life. Always remember to teach your kids that it's a competitive world out there.

Friendships

I've played team sports my entire life. To this day, I am still in contact with many of my former teammates. When you participate in sports you go through so much with your teammates. You practice and work hard together all year long. This creates a bond that no other activity can replicate. The bottom line is playing sports will develop relationships that could last a lifetime.

Taking Instruction = Better Grades

In order to be successful in life you will need to learn how to take instruction. Participating in sports will teach kids how to take orders from someone of authority. According to a study by U.C.L.A., when kids are receptive to instruction, they will be able to learn very quickly and they will be able to handle a heavy workload. Remember that sports just doesn't exercise your muscles, sports exercises your brain as well.

Winners and Losers

Playing sports will teach your kids how to win and how to lose. In the majority of sports competitive there will be a winner and a loser. Sometimes kids will be on the winning team and sometimes they will be on the losing team. Sports will teach kids how to come off a defeated and continue to work hard.

Conclusion

Parents remember that sports are a part of our culture and touch nearly everyone's life to some degree. Getting your child involved in sports has many benefits but this only happen is your kids are having fun. If you or your child is hesitant, take them to a game and let them see how the sports work and the interaction among the players. Soon they will be itching to join the fun and then becoming extraordinary will soon follow.

CHAPTER 10

OCTOBER

Each day we make deposits in the memory banks of our children." – Charles Swindoll

In October, autumn will come into full swing. Leaves will be turning colors and falling off the trees. This is a great chance to teach our children to be good neighbor and help rack some leaves or in some parts of the country shovel some snow L. Halloween is the big holiday of October, as parents let's break from tradition and give money out instead of candy. October is also the perfect month to start "leaving things better then when you have found them" with your kids.

Teach your kids to be Good neighbors

At an early age I remember one of the first thing taught in Sunday school was that in order to be a good person we must love thy neighbor. For me, after a storm ravished my neighborhood, the true love neighbors had for each other was on full display. When over 20 trees were blown over in our small cul de sac neighborhood everyone jumped into action. The men used chainsaws and axes to cut up the tree. The women and children hauled the brush to the curb and in a matter of a weekend we make sure every house was back to normal. The sad fact is that neighbors helping each other let alone even knowing each other are becoming a rare occurrence in today's society. In a 2018 study conducted by the University of Michigan found that 35 percent of Americans did not even know their neighbors name. .

We as parents must teach our children to be respectful, helpful, and kind to the people who live on our street. Here are some simple tips on how you can help your children learn to be good neighbors and by doing so becoming one step closer to be extraordinary.

A greeting and a smile go a long way

Teach your children to smile and say hello to a neighbor they see on the street. I also make sure my kids always wave when a neighbor drives by. In my neighborhood which is a mix of families and retired people, I found that a wave or a hello from a child can really put a smile on an older neighbors face.

Teach your child about boundaries, both real and invisible

If your neighbor takes special pride in their classic corvette, you definitely don't want your kids playing around it. A scooter handle could make one big scratch and ruin your neighbor's relationship with your family forever. It's also essential to teach the importance of not going in others yards without permission, for younger children sometimes this is a hard concept to understand. Also be sure to teach your kids about invisible boundaries, to me a big invisible boundary is noise and being too loud. Make sure your kids know that it is inconsiderate to other neighbors to play music loud or to scream when playing and how sounds can cross invisible boundaries.

Look for ways to be helpful

Talk to your children about being on the lookout for ways to help neighbors. If they see a neighbor driving up with groceries, perhaps they can offer to help carry the groceries into the kitchen. If your kids are old enough to shovel snow make sure they go over and help the elderly neighbor after each snow fall. As parents it is important also to lead by example if a neighbor needs help mowing their lawn or putting on new shutters offer to lend a hand. Our kids always learn from watching us!

Conclusion

There are numerous reasons you should teach your children to be good neighbors, but the single most important reason is that it makes your children better people. Remember, if the next generations learn to become better neighbors the world will be a better place.

Give cash for Halloween

This suggestion is based on one of my favorite time of the year when the leaves are changing colors, sweatshirts come out and football is on during the weekends. It's also the time for kids to dress up in their favorite costumes and going around the neighborhood getting candy. I feel we can make Halloween and our kids extraordinary by giving Cash instead of candy.

One of my fondest Halloween memories is dressing up as batman and going straight to the house on the corner of 64th Street and Grove Ave and getting a dollar bill from the nice elderly lady who lived there. This warmhearted memory made me decide to give out cash to kids instead of candy this year for Halloween. My motivation to switch from candy to cash is not just to make a lasting memory and put a smile on a kids face but also to make life healthier for kids. With nearly 1 in 3 American youth falling into the category as obese the last thing most kids need are empty calories from candy.

I suggest to everyone that they should giving each kid that comes to your door anywhere from 25 cents to $1.00 depending on your financial situation and the amount of Trick and Treaters you have. The best way to give out the money is by breaking it up with dimes and nickels so it appears the child is getting more than just one coin. I also suggest adding some words of wisdom with the money. This could be a famous quote about saving money or have something to do with being fiscally responsible.

Not only can kids benefit from handing out cash over candy for Halloween but adults can as well. According to a study by Penn State in 2014, over 63% of adults who buy Halloween candy eat it all before giving it out to the kids. Also Adults have been shown to over buy candy and find them eating the extra candy lying around from after Halloween. By giving money there is no worry about the extra calories getting into your diet from all those fun sized candy bars.

We celebrate Halloween every year with so much enthusiasm that it has become the second biggest celebration after Christmas for children around the United States. The ritual of Halloween and trick or treating have been passed on for generations, in order for us to make our kids extraordinary let's all start a new tradition and give cash over candy.

Leave something better than when you found it

My Dad had a few rules that were universally obeyed. One of them is "leave it better than you found it." It could mean a camp site or a tool that was barrowed or even a hotel room. Basically anything that does not belong to you. Leave (or return) it better than you found it. A profoundly simple rule to remind us to respect others and their property. Later in life I learned that this is the Boy Scouts motto and that many of my friends were taught this same lesson either by parents or scout leaders. Now it is our turn as parents to pass this idea down to the next generation.

Try to imagine all you and your family encounter every day. It might be people, things, or places. Each contact is the "something" you and your kids can make better then you found it: friends, grocery stores, family, co-workers, restaurants, strangers, parks, and the list continues endlessly.

Society often reverberates with the message: it's not your problem or responsibility. We need to flip the worldly perspective to say, "I will be part of the solution. How can I help?", What if we entered each day with the attitude of everything I come in contact with today, I'm going to make it better. Here are five simple examples of daily encounters made better:

1. The checkout clerk at the store – smile and ask how she is doing
2. The fast food restaurant where someone left a mess – throw away the trash with your own
3. Parking lot – push a cart to the return bin so it doesn't scratch any cars
4. Neighborhood – pull your neighbor's trash bin to the curb
5. Your children – send them off to school with encouraging words

In today's society We've heard the statements – *random acts of kindness* or *pay it forward*. This quote embraces the same connotation as leave something better then you left it . Make an impact without desiring a reward in return. Do something for others without receiving recognition. Much of the world's challenges are a result of us not all making the decision every day to leave the world just a tiny bit better than we found it. I'm not asking anyone to do anything significant or time-consuming. I'm asking you all to do little things each day that will progress us as a society. We as parents have the POWER!

CHAPTER 11

NOVEMBER

One thing I had learned from watching chimpanzees with their infants is that having a child should be fun. – Jane Goodall

November is a month that we can be thankful for our family and for the ability to vote for our leaders. Election Day is the perfect time to teach our kids to be civically engaged. This month is also a time for thanksgiving, this month is also perfect for starting some new rituals with your kids. The new ritual may be inviting someone new to your Thanksgiving feast. This month is truly about family, giving thanks and making your kids extraordinary.

Teach your kids to be civically engaged

No matter what your personal politics are, you can raise civic-minded children who are ready to help their communities and put their ideas into the world. Getting involved in civics creates empathy, forces your children to think about the future, and gives them a stake in the potential of their community. For these reasons, kids can benefit from getting engaged in civics at any level.

Here are some ways to start doing just that:

Emphasize the power of the people

While politicians have the ultimate say in some issues, it's important for children to know the power of their voices. We must teach our kids the importance of voting, rallies, boycotts, and communication. Take them to a city council meeting or a school board meeting and let them see how the audience interacts. If your child is older, consider letting them speak on an issue or invite their friends to show their support for an issue. When children are more engaged in their community, they care more about it.

Teach your children empathy

Multiple issues can affect a single person or family, but your kids likely won't face every single issue. By teaching empathy for people facing other challenges, your children can understand other viewpoints and what issues they might not have known existed. They might also come to understand that the issue they care about the most is not a priority for someone else. If they can empathize and act on issues that do not affect them directly, your children will be on their way to becoming great allies.

Encourage leadership

Your children don't need to be student body presidents or even the class president to be a leader. Maybe they are the one who creates the best games on the playground. Maybe they lead the neighbor kids in a lawn mowing business. Leadership is about making good decisions, explaining that choice, and listening when others have concerns or suggestions. Your child doesn't need to be an extrovert or planner to show others a good path forward.

Show both sides of an issue

Civic and politics can be a dirty game, but it's important for you to remain honest with your children. Let them ask you questions about politics or your community. Explain the different sides of a debate, even if you don't believe that debate should even exist. If they hear about a tragedy nearby, consider their age, but let them know what happened and why it happened.

Conclusion

Even though voting is one of the most important parts of civic engagement it's equally imperative that we as parents teach our children that their engagement should not limited to just casting a vote on a specific day. It's about taking an active role in shaping and maintaining their community as well. When this happens both our children and country will be extraordinary.

Create family rituals

Rituals help your family say, 'This is who we are and what we value as a household." Your family might not even realize that you have rituals, but even a special song at bed time can be considered a cherished family ritual.

Some rituals might have been handed down from your grandparents or other relatives, like always opening one Christmas present on Christmas eve, or going to McDonald's on Sunday mornings after church, or watching movies on Friday night. Others you might create on the fly as a family.

Your rituals might be things that no-one but your family understands. They might be:

- special morning kisses or crazy handshakes
- code words for things or special names you use for each other

- a game in the car
- a restaurant you always go to after the movies
- Your own special rules for sports.

Why rituals are important

Family rituals like meals, cultural festivals, activities, and kisses, winks or handshakes give you and your children a sense of security, identity and belonging. This is due to the fact it's something special your kids only do with a loved one and that only people in your family know the meaning. Remember that these rituals create shared memories with your children, and build/ strengthen family relationships and bonds.

Rituals can also help comfort children in unfamiliar circumstances. For example, if your child loves listening to you read a bedtime story before lights go out, this ritual will help them settle to sleep when they are in a hotel room or some other different sleeping places. According to Chase Andrews a child psychology professor from UCLA, rituals help children feel that the world is a safe and predictable place. They can be anchors that help your children feel protected in uncertain or changing times like during a family separation, or when you're moving into a different house, or after a traumatic event like a fire or flood.

Here are some suggestions you can make for creating everyday rituals that are meaningful and that will bring you closer together as a family.

Set aside certain days or times for rituals

I know a family that ice skate's together on Sundays. Saturdays are for skate classes and friends, but Sundays are for the family. Another family may set aside Sunday evenings to watch their favorite TV programs together. Neither of these activities is carved in stone, so if something comes up that's important and gets in the way, they make an exception. But they always go back to their ritual of spending Sundays together. Other families may go to church together, go to the movies or go out for dinner. But whatever it is, when your family sets aside a specific time to do an activity together, it becomes meaningful and bonds your family together.

Make dinner a ritual.

By making it a family ritual to have dinner together, you can more easily protect the time to re-connect and catch up. Talk with your kids as equals rather than as authoritarians and don't use the dinner table for reprimanding or criticizing. Instead make it fun so your kids will look forward to this special family time. Even when your kids get older and their schedules become too busy to be present at every dinner, hold on to the ritual so they are eager to get back to being together with the family.

Make bedtime a ritual.

Every child wants to go to bed feeling loved and secure and as parents we are responsible to make sure this occurs. No matter what happened during your day-even if it was frenetic and chaotic-you can tuck your children in with the same ritual every night. It makes them feel grounded and safe. Whether you read them a book, tell them a story, say prayers with them or something more creative and unique to your family, take the time to connect with them one on one and let them know how precious they are to you.

Do family projects and household tasks together.

Whether it's doing dishes, folding laundry, washing the car or taking out the garage, ask your kids to pitch in. If you've developed a family value of cooperation, participation and helping each other, it won't be difficult to get them engaged. It will teach them the spirit of kindness and the attitude of giving; pride, loyalty and not to mention the sense of team that comes from helping each other. .

Conclusion

Life today is so fast-paced and demanding, it's important that we find ways to reconnect with our children on a daily basis. Establishing family traditions helps us do just that. Traditions are those special times that bring families together, allowing us to express unity and to create bonds that last a lifetime.

Remember it's exciting to be a part of a family that hangs together and enjoys one another. You can think of your rituals as strategies that are unique to your family to help keep you close and interacting with each other in positive and healthy ways.

Invite someone to thanksgiving

Thanksgiving should be a time for an expression of gratitude, especially to God. For parents thanksgiving can be a great time to teach our children many life lessons as well. One way to do so is by inviting a new person to your Thanksgiving feast. Here are three reasons why this is a good idea:

Teaches Kindness:

Here's the obvious one, even if it bears repeating. Inviting someone into your home is a nice thing to do, regardless of the circumstances. This holiday is not about food, football, or parades – but simple human connection and sharing a meal with other people.

Broaden Your Families Social Circle:

If you've been meaning to get to know Shelly from Accounting a little bit better, and overheard that she's not going home for the holiday, it's a perfect time to put yourself out there and initiate a relationship

— platonic or otherwise. Make something happen that could turn out mutually beneficial to both of you.

Model Behavior:

If you're looking for a good teaching moment, the thanksgiving meal is a prime opportunity. Your kids can see what it feels like to offer your home to others during special occasions.

Conclusion

Thanksgiving is one of the most important holiday's that a family can celebrate. This is the perfect time to teach gratitude, something that we don't do enough of these days. Remember that family is the cornerstone of any major holiday. But Thanksgiving is also about the people close to you who are outside of your family — the other people in your life for whom you're thankful. This is a great time to invite them into your family and your traditions and at the same time help make your kids extraordinary.

CHAPTER 12

DECEMBER

Be the person you want your child to be. – Betsy Brown

The month of December brings with it snow (for many), and the celebration of Christmas. This year is a great time to instead of buying clothing buy your kids some awesome toys. Also this month is important to really take a look at how as a parent you are a role model for your children. Remember our children are much more affected by our actions then our words. So get out this month and go sledding, Christmas caroling, and shopping with your kids and be sure to finish the year off strong working on making your kids extraordinary.

Give toys instead of clothing for Christmas

This month suggestion has to do with the most magical and joyous time of the year, Christmas. Children all over the world will wake up Christmas morning with anticipation of getting that new, cool toy. However many kids will open up their presents with flurry of ribbons, paper and excitement only to find that instead of the toy they have been dreaming about is a crummy sweater. So let's make our children and Christmas more extraordinary by giving kids toys for Christmas instead of clothing.

I have personally witnessed how giving clothes to kids can suck the Christmas joy out of children. In my family we have a certain Nanna who refuses to buy my young kids toys. She will only buy them clothing (mostly pajamas and shoes). So every Christmas morning my kids are all excited to see what are in the three or four neatly wrapped presents from Nana only quickly to be heartbroken when they find out that in the beautifully wrapped box is a pair of stone washed jeans or a new red polo shirt. Their Christmas joy and excitement immediately turns to a Melancholy, "Thank You" coming out of a smile less face. The good news is there is still time before Christmas; it's not too late to buy toys.

The first start to buying that special kiddo in your life a toy over clothing is to make sure you buy the right type of toy that the special child in your life wants. In order to buy the best toy a little reconnaissance is needed to be done. The best people to help find that magnificent toy are either the kid's siblings or friends. You could cut out the middleman and go right to the source and ask the kids themselves as well if you don't mind it not being as big of a surprise. If for some reason you don't have the direct access to the family then ask a kid you know around their age what they would like.

Also be sure to take into consideration the child's personalities. Believe it or not, receiving toys can be stressful for kids, especially kids with a tendency toward apprehension. Some personality types of children want to create their own gift lists and do not enjoy receiving "off-the-list items". However some kids really enjoy spontaneity and love surprises. Remember some toys can be stressful to receive due to the fact they imply certain expectations, which a child may be uneasy about fulfilling. An example of this would be a baseball glove, this gift may make a child feel like they now have to go out for the little league team.

Conclusion:

Remember that the best part of giving gifts to kids is to see that smile on their face. So please this holiday season understanding that the children in your life's Christmas go far beyond what size they wear and are about the toys they dream about.

Though this section is based on buying toys over clothing for Christmas always remember that the thrill of a new toy doesn't last. The best gift we can give any child is our time!

Parents must be positive role models

The most important aspect of parenting is being a good role model for your children. The bottom line is that our kids are more affected by what we as parents do than by what we as parents say. According to Dr. Suzanne Gelbs, kids learn how to behave by seeing how their mothers and fathers act and by following their example. This means that children can learn both good and bad aspects of life. This is why being consistent in teaching and setting examples is very important. If you tell your child that he must not hit people and then give him a spanking as punishment for his misbehavior, your child will become confused by the mixed signals.

Below are some ideas on how to live a life that will not send mixed messages and will allow you to be the worthiest role model possible for your children, which then in-turn will lead them to become extraordinary.

Be at your best

The first step to being a parent role model is being at your best. Being at your best starts with taking good care of yourself. This means making sure you are getting enough sleep, making time to exercise, eating good food and finding healthy ways to manage negative emotions without lashing out. Depleting yourself by constantly putting other people's needs first is not a good move. That's not the kind of future you want for your kid -- so don't model it, yourself.

Model Respect

Think about how you talk about and treat your friends, family members, neighbors and even yourself. Would you say hello on the street to a stranger or hold a door for someone at the store? Your child is learning how to value other people and institutions by watching your example. This includes how you talk about school, so consider your words wisely when you're discussing your child's class, teacher or administrators. Also take in consideration that your child also takes cues on self-worth from you. Respect yourself and your child will follow your lead.

Model Communication

Do you wish your child would talk to you more? Or choose to speak instead of scream? Consider your own use of words…do you use them to hurt, criticize or argue with others, even if it's not your children? Words are a powerful thing. If you demonstrate how negative, hurtful and disrespectful language can be, your child will do the same. As parents we must be mindful of how and when you communicate—give your child your complete attention and respect their thoughts and ideas. By doing so, you are hopefully teaching your kids to do the same for you.

Model Health

Are you struggling to get your child to eat healthier foods or stop playing video games? You can't expect your kids to stopping doing it on their own! Show them how! Sit down and share healthy meals and snacks with them, reduce your own screen time and plan physical activities you can do together, like a walk in the evening or a bike ride.

Model Dependability

No parent wants to have flaky kids who let people down -- so make sure to model dependability. That means coming through for your child ("I promised that we'd going to the zoo after you cleaned up your room, so let's go!") instead of letting work or other obligations always come first. It also means coming through for friends, family, colleagues and everyone else in your life.

Model Skepticism

Children are naturally trusting and they look eagerly to their surroundings for role models. As parents we must teach our children that not all "role models" are reliable. Show them what it looks like to have a healthy skepticism and to "follow your instincts. "For example, a shoe store might say prices are lowest in town, you could privately turn to your child say: *"This store says that this is the best deal in town, but I have a hunch he might not be correct. Let's check out some other stores or online. It's important to trust your gut."*

Model Mistakes

When you as a parent do something wrong, don't make excuses. A good role model takes responsibility and admits that they did something unacceptable. It's healthy for your child to see examples of grown-ups taking responsibility for their actions -- and enforcing "consequences" to correct inappropriate behavior.

Model Uniqueness

Whatever you choose to do with your life, be proud of the person you've become, even if that means accepting some ridicule. We, as parents must be role models who won't pretend to be someone they are not, and won't be fake just to suit other people.

Model well roundedness

Great role models aren't just "teachers." They are constant learners, who challenge themselves to get out of their comfort zones, and surround themselves with smarter people. When our kids see that their role model can be many things, they will learn to stretch themselves in order to be successful.

Conclusion

Keep this in mind: teaching by example is often easier and more effective than forcing children to obey rules by scaring, threatening, or tempting them with rewards. I think of the example of the mother who screams at her children to, "Stop yelling!" She might really want them to stop, but is she teaching them how to effectively communicate or just modeling the same bad behavior?

Remember it's not about being a perfect parent or role model rather, it's about being mindful that your words and actions are being watched and absorbed by your children. This is a GOOD thing for us parents, because it means that every day we have a chance to help our children become extraordinary.

Final Thoughts

"Mothers and fathers shape the future of the world, because they shape their children"

Parenting is the most important issue facing our society. According to Dr. Ann Harrison of Harvard's school of sociology, the actions of parents is single largest variable implicated in childhood illnesses and accidents; teenage pregnancy and substance misuse; truancy, school disruption, and underachievement; child abuse; employability; juvenile crime; and mental illness. These are all serious issues that can negatively affect the life of a child well into adulthood. This is why it is so important that you use the suggestions from this book to raise extraordinary kids.

"Given the importance of parenting it is a sad fact that most kids spend an average of 41 hours per week in front of some type of screen (TV, computer, phone) but they only spend 7 hour per week with their parents." (Administration for children and families annual report, 2019) Unfortunately, many parents either don't or are afraid to spend one-on-one time with their children. Besides missing out on the fun, parents miss out on bonding time and a chance to establish emotional intimacy with their kiddos. Please take the time and use the suggestions from this book to spend more time with your kids every chance you get.

As parents we must make sure we are looking at the bigger picture of how we raise our children will impact on what type of adults they become. According to the famous child phycologist Mary Ainsworth, the future of our society is shaped now by how we rear our children, and we need to take this duty more seriously. Society must admit the importance of being a parent. Moms and dads should not feel they are wasting their talents if they stay home to raise children. I personally feel much more needed and fulfilled as a stay at home dad than I have at any other life endeavor.

Remember that the world will only be as strong as its families, and families will only be as strong as its parents. Peace on our planet begins with peace in the home. The sustainable development of our societies depends on the work of moms and dads collaborating to help each other raise not just kids but fully and integrally developed adults. "Respect for human dignity and rights flows much more easily from the school of familial love" (Erickson 1967). Since the future of the world passes by way of families today, parents and future parents need to be prepared, supported and encouraged to carry out their indispensable role, individually and mutually as a committed dynamic duo through building strong parenting skills.

Parenting skills assist parents in leading children into healthy adulthood, influencing their development, and maintaining their negative and positive behaviors. One of the goals of this book is to build upon parenting skills. As a parent other then has read this book you should try every day to find a way to strengthen the following:

1. Maintain consistency: Parents that institute regular routines see benefits in their children's behavioral patterns;
2. Utilize resources available to them: This could be in written form such as this book or even places like nature centers or other places that promote learning
3. Take an interest in their child's educational and early developmental needs
4. Keep open lines of communication about what their child is seeing, learning, and doing, and how these things are affecting them.
5. Parent-child relationship skills: quality time spent positive communications and delighted show of affection.

6. Encouraging desirable behavior: praise and encouragement, nonverbal attention, facilitating engaging activities.
7. Teaching skills and behaviors: being a good example, incidental teaching, communicating logical incentives and consequences.
8. Anticipating and planning: advanced planning and preparation for readying the child for challenges, finding out engaging and age-appropriate developmental activities

The bottom line is as parents in order to see our kids succeed we must be involved in our children's life. Being an involved parent takes time and is hard work, and it often means rethinking and rearranging your priorities. It frequently means sacrificing what you want to do for what your child needs to do. We must be there mentally as well as physically.

Parents can sometimes forget how important we are in the lives of our children.

We have so much control we have in shaping their confidence and self-image. And it all starts with trust, with believing a child is capable, even though setbacks, surprises and all the complications that come with growing up.

Trust empowers kids, whether it's in the classroom or in the world at large, and the process of developing trust starts earlier than you think. Infants who are securely attached to their parents — who feel they can trust and depend on them — avoid many behavioral, social, and psychological problems that can arise later. A child's fundamental sense of security in the world is based on their caregiver being someone they can rely upon.

Remember, trust is mutual.

The degree to which your children can trust you will become reflected in their own ability to trust. Studies show that children rated as less trustworthy by their teacher's exhibit higher levels of aggression and lower levels of "prosocial behavior" such as collaborating and sharing. Distrust in children has also been associated with their social withdrawal and loneliness.

If we don't feel trusted when we're kids — or if there isn't anyone close to us we can trust — we have difficulty getting over it. We grow up thinking we're not trustworthy, and we accept it as a character trait. Like Michael, we become what we think we are, and we can suffer for it.

Always laugh together, spend time together, and connect positively every single day. Whether it's sitting down to play a fun board game, going for a bike ride, cooking, watching a movie, or just reading a good book together (or reading different books side-by-side, if your child is older), good parents spend time doing something fun and connecting with their kids in small and large ways every single day. Time truly flies when we are involved in our children's life. After all Mothers and Fathers shape the future of the world, because they shape their children.

Bonus

Father forgets for the 21st century:
A tribute to Livingston Larned's poem
By
Dr. Jon Kester

Father forgets for the 21st century
By Dr. Jon Kester

Listen Daughter, I am saying this as you are fast asleep, one little hand crumpled under your Disney Princess pillow and another around your favorite stuffed animal. I have come into your room alone. Just a few minutes ago, as I sat reading my emails, an overwhelming wave of remorse swept over me. Guilty, I came to your bedside.

There are things which I am thinking, daughter; your actions have made me angry. I yelled at you for using way to much shampoo in the shower. I got irritated at you for wanting to wear your favorite shirt that looked faded instead of all the nice new clothes in your closet. I called out furiously when you left your wet towel in the middle of the hall way.

At breakfast I found fault, too. You spilled milk all over the counter. You dropped your cereal all over the floor. You forgot to wash your hands after eating and gave me a hug which got my shirt all dirty. As you ran out the door to get on the bus you turned and waved and yelled,

"Goodbye, Daddy!" I frowned, and said in reply, "keep those new shoes I just bought you clean!"

Then it began all over again late this afternoon. As I drove up the road I noticed you using the iPad listening to music outside. There was dirt on the screen. I humiliated you in front of you friends Lucy and Hannah by yelling at you and sending you to have a "time out" in the house. An IPad is expensive, and if you had to buy one you would be more careful!

Do you remember later, when I was checking my emails, how you came nervously, with sort of a hurt look in your eyes? I glanced up over my laptop, impatient at the interruption; you hesitated at the door. "What is it that you want?" I snapped. You said nothing, but ran across the room, threw your arms around my neck and kissed me, and said "Good night daddy. I love you. Then you were gone, quickly running up the stairs.

Well, daughter, it was shortly afterwards that I closed my laptop and a terrible sickening fear came over me. What has habit been doing to me? The habit of finding fault, or criticizing; this was my reward to you for being a child. It was not that I did not love you: it was that I expected too much of you. I had expectations for you of those of an adult.

There is so much that was good, fine and true in your character. The little heart of yours was as big as a football stadium. This was shown by your spontaneous impulse to rush in and kiss me good night. Nothing else mattered tonight.

Daughter, I have come to your beside in the darkness, I have knelt there, ashamed! I know that you would not understand these things which I have told you in the morning hours. Tomorrow I will be a real daddy! I will befriend you, suffer when you suffer and laugh when you laugh. I will bite my tongue when impatient words come. I will keep saying as if it were a ritual: "She is just a little girl" I am afraid I have envisioned you as an adult.

Yet as I see you now, daughter, lying asleep in your bed, I see that you are still my baby. It seems like just yesterday you were a newborn in your mother's arms, looking up at me with a crinkled forehead. I have asked too much, too much!

Instead of condemning and criticizing our children, perhaps would it be better to try to understand them, to try to figure out why they do what they do. That's a lot more beneficial than criticism; and it produces sympathy, tolerance and kindness, rather than contempt...!!!

BIBLIOGRAPHY

Abidin, R. R. (1992). The determinants of parenting behavior. *Journal of Clinical Child Psychology, 21*(4), 407-412. https://doi.org/10.1207/s15374424jccp2104_12

Abidin, R. R. (2012) *Parenting Stress Index-4 professional manual.* Lutz, FL: PAR, Inc.

Amato; Howard & Reeves (2018) Father involvement and self-reportparenting of children with attention deficit-hyperactivity disorder. *Journal of Consulting and Clinical Psychology, 65*(2), 337-342. doi:10.1037/0022-006X.65.2.337

Åsberg, K. K., Vogel, J. J., & Bowers, C. A. (2008). Exploring correlates and predictors of stress in parents of children who are deaf: Implications of perceived social support and mode of communication. *Journal of Child and Family Studies, 17*(4), 486-499. doi:10.1007/s10826-007-9169-7

Bailey, C. L., & Rose, V. C. (2011). Examining teachers' perceptions of twice exceptional students: Overview of a qualitative exploration. *Ideas and Research You Can Use: VISTAS,* 1-12.

Baldwin, K., Brown, R. T., & Milan, M. A. (1995). Predictors of stress in caregivers of attention deficit hyperactivity disordered children. *American Journal of Family Therapy, 23*(2), 149–160. doi:10.1080/01926189508251345

Bandura, A. (1977). Self-efficacy: Toward a unifying theory of behavioral change. *Psychological Review,*

Banks, M. L., (2018). The impact of complex trauma and depression on parenting: An exploration of mediating risk and protective factors. *Child Maltreatment, 8*(4), 334-349. https://doi.org/10.1177/1077559503257106

Becker, J. (2016). Clutter Free with Kids: *55*, 83–96.

Belsky, J., Crnic, K., & Woodworth, S. (1995). Personality and parenting: Exploring the mediating role of transient mood and daily hassles. *Journal of Personality, 63*(4), 905-929. https://doi.org/10.1111/j.1467-6494.1995.tb00320.x

Berson, M.L (2015). The advocacy experiences of parents of elementary age, twice-exceptional children. *Gifted Child Quarterly, 37*(1), 1-16. https://doi.org/10.1177/0016986215569275

Bianco, M., & Leech, N. L. (2010). Twice-exceptional learners: Effects of teacher preparation and disability labels on gifted referrals. *Teacher Education and Special Education, 33*(4), 319-334. https://doi.org/10.1177/0888406409356392

Blanche, E. I., Diaz, J., Barretto, T., & Cermak, S. A. (2015). Caregiving experiences of Latino families with children with autism spectrum disorder. *American Journal of Occupational Therapy, 69*(5), 1-11. https://doi.org/10.5014/ajot.2015.017848

Bream, A.S. (2017). *Completing your qualitative dissertation: A road map from beginning to end.* Thousand Oaks, CA: Sage Publications. 151

Cambridge, M. (2015). Mothers' and fathers' attributions and beliefs in families of girls and boys with attention-deficit/hyperactivity disorder. *Child Psychiatry & Human Development, 39*(1), 85-99. doi:10.1007/s10578-007-0073-6

Comallie-Caplan, L. (2012). The apple doesn't fall far from the tree: Gifted parents parenting gifted children. *SENGVine Gifted Adult Edition.* Retrieved from https://sengifted.org/archives/articles/gifted-parents-parenting-gifted-children

Covington, M. K.,(2013). Parenting stress among caregivers of children with chronic illness: A systematic review. *Journal of Pediatric Psychology, 38*(8), 809-828. https://doi.org/10.1093/jpepsy/jst049

Creasey, G., & Reese, M. (1996). Mothers' and fathers' perceptions of parenting hassles: Associations with psychological symptoms, nonparenting hassles, and child behavior problems. *Journal of Applied Developmental Psychology, 17*, 393-406. https://doi.org/10.1016/s0193-3973(96)90033-7

Creswell, J. W. (2007). *Qualitative inquiry & research design: Choosing among five traditions.* Thousand Oaks, CA: Sage Publications.

Crnic, K., & Greenberg, M. (1990). Minor parenting stress with young children. *Child Development, 54*, 209–217. https://doi.org/10.2307/1130770

Cross, J. R., & Cross, T. L. (2015). Clinical and mental health issues in counseling the gifted individual. *Journal of Counseling & Development, 93*(2), 163-172. https://doi.org/10.1002/j.1556-6676.2015.00192.x
152

Cuva, A. (2014). Traversing the uncharted arena of computer assisted qualitative data analysis software: Mapping out QDA Miner 4.1 as a first-time user. *The Qualitative Report, 19*(19), 1-4.

Daniels, S., & Piechowski, M. M. (Eds.) (2009). *Living with intensity: Understanding the excitability, sensitivity, and emotional development of gifted children, adolescents, and adults.* Scottsdale, AZ: Gifted Potential Press.

Dare, L., & Nowicki, E. A. (2015). Twice-exceptionality: Parents' perspectives on 2E identification. *Roeper Review, 37*, 208-218. doi: 10.1080/02783193.2015.1077911

Deater-Deckard, K. (2004). *Parenting stress.* New Haven, CT: Yale University Press.

Deault, L. C. (2010). A systematic review of parenting in relation to the development of comorbidities and functional impairments in children with attentiondeficit/hyperactivity disorder (ADHD). *Child Psychiatry and Human Development, 41*(2), 168-192. doi:10.1007/s10578-009-0159-4

Detmer, James. (2018). Responsible fathering: An overview and conceptual framework. *Journal of Marriage and Family, 60*, 277-292. doi:10.2307/353848

Duhigg, Charles(2009). The power of Habit: Implications for parent–child relationships and prevention research. *Clinical Child and Family Psychology Review, 12*(3), 255-270.
153

Elman,.A. J, (2011). Beyond internal and external: A dyadic theory of relational attributions. *The Academy of Management Review, 36*(4), 731-753. https://doi.org/10.5465/amr.2011.65554734

Engram, H. Thomas. (2020). Relationships between maternal parenting stress and child disruptive behavior. *Child & Family Behavior Therapy, 14*(4), 1-9. https://doi.org/10.1300/j019v14n04_01

Fischer, M. (1990). Parenting stress and the child with attention deficit hyperactivity disorder. *Journal of Clinical Child Psychology, 19*(4), 337–346.
https://doi.org/10.1207/s15374424jccp1904_5

Folkman, S., Lazarus, R. S., Gruen, R. J., & DeLongis, A. (1986). Appraisal, coping, health status, and psychological symptoms. *Journal of Personality and Social Psychology, 50*(3), 571-579. doi:10.1037/0022-3514.50.3.571

Foster, S. David. (2018). Finding and serving twice exceptional students: Using triaged comprehensive assessment and protections of the law. In S. B. Kaufman
(Ed.) *Twice exceptional: Supporting and educating bright and creative students with learning difficulties* (pp. 19-47). New York, NY: Oxford University Press.

Gelbs, J.S. (2003). Understanding reliability and validity in qualitative research. *The Qualitative Report, 8*(4), 597-606.

Grant, B. A., & Piechowski, M. M. (1999) Theories and the good: Toward child-centered gifted education. *Gifted Child Quarterly, 43*(1), 4-12.
https://doi.org/10.1177/001698629904300102
154

Gross, M. (2004). *Exceptionally gifted children* (2nd Ed.). London, England: Routledge Falmer.

Grossman, F. K., Pollack, W. S., & Golding, E. (1988). Fathers and children: Predicting the quality and quantity of fathering. *Developmental Psychology, 24*(1), 82-91. doi:10.1037/0012-1649.24.1.82

Gupta, V. B. (2007). Comparison of parenting stress in different developmental disabilities. *Journal of Developmental & Physical Disabilities, 19*(4), 417–425. doi:10.1007/s10882-007-9060-x

Harrison J. A. (2018). Maternal positive parenting style is associated with better functioning in hyperactive/inattentive preschool children. *Infant and Child Development, 20*(2), 148–161. doi:10.1002/icd.682

Hurt, Karin. (2019). What we know about the early selection and training of leaders. *Teachers College Record, 40*, 575-592. Individuals with Disabilities Education Improvement Act of 2004, 108 U.S.C. §§ 108- 446 (West, 2004).

Johnston, C., & Mash, E. J. (2001). Families of children with attentiondeficit/hyperactivity disorder: Review and recommendations for future research. *Clinical Child and Family Psychology Review, 4*(3), 183–207. doi:10.1023/A:1017592030434 155

Jolly, J. L., & Matthews, M. S. (2012). A critique of the literature on parenting gifted learners. *Journal for the Education of the Gifted, 35*(3), 259-290. https://doi.org/10.1177/0162353212451703

Jolly, J. L., Matthews, M. S., & Nester, J. (2012). Homeschooling the gifted: A parent's perspective. *Gifted Child Quarterly, 57*(2), 121-134. https://doi.org/10.1177/0016986212469999

Kadesjö, C., Stenlund, H., Wels, P., Gillberg, C., & Hägglöf, B. (2002). Appraisals of stress in child-rearing in Swedish mothers of pre-schoolers with ADHD: A questionnaire study. *European*

Child & Adolescent Psychiatry, 11(4), 185–195. doi:10.1007/s00787-002-0281-3

Kane, M. (2013) Parent lore: Collected stories of asynchronous development. In C. S. Neville, M. M. Piechowski, & S. S. Tolan (Eds.) *Off the charts: Asynchrony and the gifted child* (pp. 226-259). Unionville, NY: Royal Fireworks Press.

Karpinski, R. I., Kolb, A. M. K., Tetreault, N. A., & Borowski, T. B. (2017). High intelligence: A risk factor for psychological and physiological overexcitabilities.
Intelligence, 66(1), 8-23. https://doi.org/10.1016/j.intell.2017.09.001

Kaufman, S. B. (Ed.) (2018). *Twice exceptional: Supporting and educating brought and creative students with learning difficulties.* New York, NY: Oxford University Press.

156

Kazdin, A. E., & Wassell, G. (2000). Predictors of barriers to treatment and therapeutic change in outpatient therapy for antisocial children and their families. *Mental Health Services Research, 2*(1), 27-40.

Kazdin, A. E., & Whitley, M. K. (2003). Treatment of parental stress to enhance therapeutic change among children referred for aggressive and antisocial behavior. *Journal of Consulting and Clinical Psychology, 71*(3), 504-515.
https://doi.org/10.1037/0022-006x.71.3.504

Kearney, K. (2013). Life in the asynchronous family. In C. S. Neville, M. M. Piechowski, & S. S. Tolan (Eds.) *Off the charts: Asynchrony and the gifted child* (pp. 211-225). Unionville, NY: Royal Fireworks Press.

Knott, L. J. (2020). Predictors of boys' ADHD symptoms from early to middle childhood: The role of father–child and mother–child interactions. *Journal of Abnormal Child Psychology, 40*(4), 569-581. doi:10.1007/s10802-011-9586-3

Lamb, M. E. (2010). *The role of the father in child development.* Hoboken, NJ: John Wiley & Sons.

Lange, G., Sheerin, D., Carr, A., Dooley, B., Barton, V., Marshall, D.,... Doyle, M. (2005). Family factors associated with attention deficit

hyperactivity disorder and emotional disorders in children. *Journal of Family Therapy, 27*(1), 76–96.
doi:10.1111/j.1467-6427.2005.00300.x
157

Latz, A. O., & Adams, C. M. (2011). Critical differentiation and the twice oppressed:
Social class and giftedness. *Journal for the Education of the Gifted, 34*(5), 773-
789. https://doi.org/10.1177/0162353211417339

Lazarus, R. S. (2006). *Stress and emotion.* New York, NY: Springer Publishing.

Lazarus, R. S., & Folkman, S. (1984). *Stress, appraisal, and coping.* New York, NY:
Springer Publishing Company.

Lombardi, D. V. (2004). *Different minds: Gifted children with AD/HD, Asperger syndrome, and other learning deficits.* London, England: Jessica Kingsley Publishers.

Makel, M. C., Kell, H. J., Lubinski, D., Putallaz, M., & Benbow, C. P. (2016). When lightning strikes twice: Profoundly gifted, profoundly accomplished.
Psychological Science, 27(7), 1004-1018.
https://doi.org/10.1177/0956797616644735

Manning, J., & Kunkel, A. (2014). Making meaning of meaning-making research: Using qualitative research for studies of social and personal relationships. *Journal of Social and Personal Relationships, 31*(4), 433-441.
https://doi.org/10.1177/0265407514525890

Marshall.A.S (2019). Determinants of parenting stress: Illustrations from families of hyperactive children and families of physically abused children.
Journal of Clinical Child Psychology, 19(4), 313-328.
doi:10.1207/s15374424jccp1904_3
158

Maxwell, E. (1998). "I can do it myself!" Reflections on early self-efficacy. *Roeper*

Review, 20(3), 183-187. https://doi.org/10.1080/02783199809553888

McCleary, L. (2002). Parenting adolescents with attention deficit hyperactivity disorder:

Analysis of the literature for social work practice. *Health & Social Work, 27*(4),

285–292. doi:10.1093/hsw/27.4.285

Merrill, J. (2012). *If this is a gift, can I send it back?: Surviving in the land of the gifted and twice exceptional.* Ashland, OR: GHF Press.

Mueller, A. K., Fuermaier, A. B., Koerts, J., & Tucha, L. (2012). Stigma in attention deficit hyperactivity disorder. *ADHD attention deficit and hyperactivity disorders,*

4(3), 101-114.

Miller, J. B., & Stiver, I. P. (1997). *The healing connection: How women form relationships in therapy and in life.* Boston, MA: Beacon Press.

Modesto-Lowe, V., Danforth, J. S., & Brooks, D. (2008). ADHD: Does parenting style matter? *Clinical Pediatrics, 47*(9), 865–872. doi:10.1177/0009922808319963

Morelock, M. J. (1992). Giftedness: The view from within. *Understanding Our Gifted, 4*(3), 11-15.

Morelock, M. J. (1996). On the nature of giftedness and talent: Imposing order on chaos. *Roeper Review, 19*(1), 4-12. https://doi.org/10.1080/02783199609553774

Morgan, J., Robinson, D., & Aldridge, J. (2002). Parenting stress and externalizing child behaviour. *Child & Family Social Work, 7*(3), 219-225.

https://doi.org/10.1046/j.1365-2206.2002.00242.x

159

Moustakas, C. (1994). *Phenomenological research methods.* Thousand Oaks, CA: Sage Publications.

Mudrak, J. (2011). 'He was born that way': Parental constructions of giftedness. *High Ability Studies, 22*(2), 199-217. https://doi.org/10.1080/13598139.2011.622941

Neece, C. L., Green, S. A., & Baker, B. L. (2012). Parenting stress and child behavior problems: A transactional relationship across time.

American Journal on Intellectual and Developmental Disabilities,
117(1), 48-66.
https://doi.org/10.1352/1944-7558-117.1.48

Neumann, L. C. (2008). No one said it was easy: Challenges of parenting twiceexceptional children. In Gosfield, M. (Ed.), *Expert approaches to support gifted learners: Professional perspectives, best practices and positive solutions* (pp. 269–276). Minneapolis, MN: Free Spirit Press.

Neville, C. S., Piechowski, M. M., & Tolan, S. S. (Eds.) (2013) *Off the charts: Asynchrony and the gifted child.* Unionville, NY: Royal Fireworks Press.

No Child Left Behind (NCLB) Act of 2001, 20 U.S.C.A. § 6301 et seq. (West, 2003).

Oakland, J. (2018). Boys will be boys: Fathers' perspectives on ADHD symptoms, diagnosis, and drug treatment. *Harvard Review of Psychiatry, 11*(6), 308-316.
doi:10.1080/714044393

Oswald, I. (2014). Doing their jobs: Mothering with Ritalin in a culture of mother-blame.
Social Science & Medicine, 59(6), 1193-1205.
https://doi.org/10.1016/j.socscimed.2004.01.011

Owens, David. (2018). A structural modeling approach to the understanding of parenting stress. *Journal of Clinical Child Psychology, 29*(4), 615-625.
https://doi.org/10.1207/s15374424jccp2904_13

Palmer R.M. (2013). The influence of primary caregivers in fostering success in twice-exceptional children. *Gifted Child Quarterly, 57*(4), 263-274. https://doi.org/10.1177/0016986213500068

Palson, Diana. (2011). Meaning, coping, and health and well-being. In S. Folkman (Ed.) *Oxford handbook of stress, health, and coping* (pp. 227-241). New York, NY:
Oxford University Press.
160

Patton, M.Q. (2014). *Qualitative research & evaluation methods: Integrating theory and practice.* Thousand Oaks, CA: SAGE Publications.

Pelham, W., & Lang, A. (1999). Can your children drive you to drink? Stress and parenting in adults interacting with children with ADHD. *Alcohol Research & Health, 23*(4), 292–298.

Pew Study. (2018). Myth 17: Gifted and talented individuals do not have unique social and emotional needs. *Gifted Child Quarterly, 53*(4), 280-282. https://doi.org/10.1177/0016986209346946

Peterman,A. J. (2016). Bullying and the gifted: Victims, perpetrators, prevalence, and effects. *Gifted Child Quarterly, 50*(2), 148-168. https://doi.org/10.1177/001698620605000206

Petit,J.J. (2020). Where's poppa? The relative lack of attention to the role of fathers in child and adolescent psychopathology. *American Psychologist, 47*(5), 656-664. doi:10.1037/0003-066X.47.5.656

Piechowski, M. M. (2014). *"Mellow out," they say. If I only could: Intensities and sensitivities of the young and bright* (2nd ed.). Unionville, NY: Royal Fireworks Press.

Podolski, C. L., & Nigg, J. T. (2001). Parent stress and coping in relation to child ADHD severity and associated child disruptive behavior problems. *Journal of Clinical Child Psychology, 30*(4), 503–513. https://doi.org/10.1207/s15374424jccp3004_07
161

Postma, M. (2017). *The inconvenient student: Critical issues in the identification and education of twice-exceptional students.* Unionville, NY: Royal Fireworks Press.

Power, T. G., & Hill, L. G. (2010). Individual differences in appraisal of minor, potentially stressful events: A cluster analytic approach. *Cognition and Emotion, 24*(7), 1081-1094. https://doi.org/10.1080/02699930903122463

Prior, S. (2013). Transition and students with twice exceptionality. *Australasian Journal of Special Education, 37*(1), 19. https://doi.org/10.1017/jse.2013.3

Randall, A. K., & Bodenmann, G. (2009). The role of stress on close relationships and marital satisfaction. *Clinical Psychology Review, 29*, 105-115.
https://doi.org/10.1016/j.cpr.2008.10.004

Raphael, J. L., Zhang, Y. Y., Liu, H. H., & Giardino, A. P. (2010). Parenting stress in US families: Implications for paediatric healthcare utilization. *Child: Care, Health and Development, 36*(2), 216-224. doi:10.1111/j.1365-2214.2009.01052.x

Robertson S.A. (2018). An operational definition of twiceexceptional learners: Implications and applications. *Gifted Child Quarterly, 58*(3),
217-230. https://doi.org/10.1177/0016986214534976

Saldaña, J. (2009). *The coding manual for qualitative researchers.* Thousand Oaks, CA:
Sage Publications.

Sheeran, T., Marvin, R. S., & Pianta, R. (1997). Mothers' resolution of their childs's diagnosis and self-reported measures of parenting stress, marital relations, and 162 social support. *Journal of Pediatric Psychology, 22*(2), 197-212.
https://doi.org/10.1093/jpepsy/22.2.197

Silverman, L. K. (1990). Social and emotional education of the gifted: The discoveries of Leta Hollingworth. *Roeper Review, 12*(3), 171-178. https://doi.org/10.1080/02783199009553265

Silverman, L. K. (1997). The construct of asynchronous development. *Peabody Journal of Education, 72*(3-4), 36-58. https://doi. org/10.1207/s15327930pje7203&4_3

Silverman, L. K. (1998). Through the lens of giftedness. *Roeper Review, 20*(3), 204-210.

Silverman, L. K. (2002). Asynchronous development. In M. Neihart, S. M. Reis, N. M. Robinson, & S. M. Moon (Eds.) *The social and emotional development of gifted children: What do we know?* (pp. 31-50). Waco, TX: Prufrock Press.

Silverman, L. K.. & Kearney, K. (1989). Parents of the extraordinarily gifted. *Advanced Development, 1,* 41-56.

Silverman, L. K., & Miller, N. B. (2009). A feminine perspective of giftedness. In L. V.

Silvestri.R.K. (2018). Stress, coping, and social support processes: Where are we? What next? *Journal of Health and Social Behavior*, (Extra issue), 53-79. https://doi.org/10.2307/2626957

Shavinina (Ed.), *International handbook on giftedness* (pp. 99-128). Amsterdam:

Netherlands: Springer.

Singer, L. (2000). If giftedness = asynchronous development, then gifted/special needs = asynchrony3. In K. Kay (Ed.), *Uniquely gifted: Identifying and meeting the needs of twice-exceptional students* (pp. 44-46). Gilsum, NH: Avocus Publishing Inc.

163

Spicer, P. (2007). Commentary: From fathering to parenting and back again. *Applied Developmental Science, 11*(4), 203-204. doi:10.1080/10888690701762084

Spratt, E. G., Saylor, C. F., & Macias, M. M. (2007). Assessing parenting stress in multiple samples of children with special needs (CSN). *Families, Systems, & Health, 25*(4), 435-449. doi:10.1037/1091-7527.25.4.435

Stewart, D., & Mickunas, A. (1974). *Exploring phenomenology: A guide to the field and its literature.* Athens, OH: Ohio University Press.

Theule, J., Wiener, J., Rogers, M. A., & Marton, I. (2011). Predicting parenting stress in families of children with ADHD: Parent and contextual factors. *Journal of Child and Family Studies, 20*(5), 640–647. doi:10.1007/s10826-010-9439-7

164

Tieso, C. L. (2007). Patterns of overexcitabilities in identified gifted students and their parents: A hierarchical model. *Gifted Child Quarterly, 51*(1), 11-22. https://doi.org/10.1177/0016986206296657

Trépanier, C. (2015). *Educating your gifted child: How one public school teacher embraced homeschooling.* Olympia, WA: GHF Press.

Tzang, R. F., Chang, Y. C., & Liu, S. I. (2009). The association between children's ADHD subtype and parenting stress and parental symptoms. *International Journal of Psychiatry in Clinical Practice, 13*(4), 318-325. https://doi.org/10.3109/13651500903094567

Van der Oord, S., Bögels, S. M., & Peijnenburg, D. (2012). The effectiveness of mindfulness training for children with ADHD and mindful parenting for their parents. *Journal of Child and Family Studies, 21*(1), 139-147. https://doi.org/10.1007/s10826-011-9457-0

Van de Weijer-Bergsma, E., Formsma, A. R., de Bruin, E. I., & Bögels, S. M. (2012). The effectiveness of mindfulness training on behavioral problems and attentional functioning in adolescents with ADHD. *Journal of Child and Family Studies, 21*(5), 775-787. https://doi.org/10.1007/s10826-011-9531-7
165

Van Manen, M. (1990). *Researching lived experience: Human science for an action sensitive pedagogy*. Albany, NY: State University of New York Press.

Van Manen, M. (2014). *Phenomenology of practice: Meaning-giving methods in phenomenological research and writing*. Walnut Creek, CA: Left Coast Press.

Vialle, W. (2017). Supporting giftedness in families: A resources perspective. *Journal for the Education of the Gifted, 40*(4), 372-393. https://doi.org/10.1177/0162353217734375

Webb, J., Meckstroth, E., & Tolan, S. (1982). *Guiding the gifted child: A practical source for parents and teachers*. Columbus, OH: Ohio Psychology Publishing Company.

Weiner, B. (1985). An attributional theory of achievement motivation and emotion. *Psychological Review, 92*(4), 548-573. doi:10.1037/0033-295X.92.4.548

Weiner, B. (2000). Intrapersonal and interpersonal theories of motivation from an attributional perspective. *Educational Psychology Review, 12*(1), 1-14.

Wells, C. (2017). The primary importance of the inner experience of giftedness.
Advanced Development, 16, 95-113.

Whalen, C. K., Odgers, C. L., Reed, P. L., & Henker, B. (2011). Dissecting daily distress in mothers of children with ADHD: An electronic diary study. *Journal of Family Psychology, 25*(3), 402. https://doi.org/10.1037/a0023473

Yehuda, R., Halligan, S. L., & Grossman, R. (2001). Childhood trauma and risk for PTSD: Relationship to intergenerational effects of trauma, parental PTSD, and

166

cortisol excretion. *Development and Psychopathology, 13,* 733-753. https://doi.org/10.1017/s0954579401003170

167

Printed in the United States
by Baker & Taylor Publisher Services